# Portfolio Theory and Risk Management

With its emphasis on examples, exercises and calculations, this book suits advanced undergraduates as well as postgraduates and practitioners. It provides a clear treatment of the scope and limitations of mean-variance portfolio theory and introduces popular modern risk measures. Proofs are given in detail, assuming only modest mathematical background, but with attention to clarity and rigour. The discussion of VaR and its more robust generalizations, such as AVaR, brings recent developments in risk measures within range of some undergraduate courses and includes a novel discussion of reducing VaR and AVaR by means of hedging techniques.

A moderate pace, careful motivation and more than 70 exercises give students confidence in handling risk assessments in modern finance. Solutions and additional materials for instructors are available at www.cambridge.org/9781107003675.

MACIEJ J. CAPIŃSKI is an Associate Professor in the Faculty of Applied Mathematics at AGH University of Science and Technology in Kraków, Poland. His interests include mathematical finance, financial modelling, computer-assisted proofs in dynamical systems and celestial mechanics. He has authored 10 research publications, one book, and supervised over 30 MSc dissertations, mostly in mathematical finance.

EKKEHARD KOPP is Emeritus Professor of Mathematics at the University of Hull, where he taught courses at all levels in analysis, measure and probability, stochastic processes and mathematical finance between 1970 and 2007. His editorial experience includes service as founding member of the Springer Finance series (1998–2008) and the Cambridge University Press AIMS Library Series. He has taught in the UK, Canada and South Africa and he has authored more than 50 research publications and five books.

## Mastering Mathematical Finance

Mastering Mathematical Finance is a series of short books that cover all core topics and the most common electives offered in Master's programmes in mathematical or quantitative finance. The books are closely coordinated and largely self-contained, and can be used efficiently in combination but also individually.

The MMF books start financially from scratch and mathematically assume only undergraduate calculus, linear algebra and elementary probability theory. The necessary mathematics is developed rigorously, with emphasis on a natural development of mathematical ideas and financial intuition, and the readers quickly see real-life financial applications, both for motivation and as the ultimate end for the theory. All books are written for both teaching and self-study, with worked examples, exercises and solutions.

[DMFM]    *Discrete Models of Financial Markets*,
          Marek Capiński, Ekkehard Kopp

[PF]      *Probability for Finance*,
          Ekkehard Kopp, Jan Malczak, Tomasz Zastawniak

[SCF]     *Stochastic Calculus for Finance*,
          Marek Capiński, Ekkehard Kopp, Janusz Traple

[BSM]     *The Black–Scholes Model*,
          Marek Capiński, Ekkehard Kopp

[PTRM]    *Portfolio Theory and Risk Management*,
          Maciej J. Capiński, Ekkehard Kopp

[NMFC]    *Numerical Methods in Finance with C++*,
          Maciej J. Capiński, Tomasz Zastawniak

[SIR]     *Stochastic Interest Rates*,
          Daragh McInerney, Tomasz Zastawniak

[CR]      *Credit Risk*,
          Marek Capiński, Tomasz Zastawniak

[FE]      *Financial Econometrics*,
          Marek Capiński

[SCAF]    *Stochastic Control Applied to Finance*,
          Szymon Peszat, Tomasz Zastawniak

**Series editors** Marek Capiński, *AGH University of Science and Technology, Kraków*; Ekkehard Kopp, *University of Hull*; Tomasz Zastawniak, *University of York*

# Portfolio Theory and Risk Management

MACIEJ J. CAPIŃSKI

*AGH University of Science and Technology, Kraków, Poland*

EKKEHARD KOPP

*University of Hull, Hull, UK*

CAMBRIDGE
UNIVERSITY PRESS

# CAMBRIDGE
## UNIVERSITY PRESS

University Printing House, Cambridge CB2 8BS, United Kingdom

Cambridge University Press is part of the University of Cambridge.

It furthers the University's mission by disseminating knowledge in the pursuit of education, learning and research at the highest international levels of excellence.

www.cambridge.org
Information on this title: www.cambridge.org/9781107003675

© Maciej J. Capiński and Ekkehard Kopp 2014

First published 2014

*A catalogue record for this publication is available from the British Library*

*Library of Congress Cataloguing in Publication data*
Capiński, Maciej J.
Portfolio theory and risk management / Maciej J. Capiński, AGH University of Science and Technology, Kraków, Poland, Ekkehard Kopp, University of Hull, Hull, UK.
pages cm – (Mastering mathematical finance)
Includes bibliographical references and index.
ISBN 978-1-107-00367-5 (Hardback) – ISBN 978-0-521-17714-6 (Paperback)
1. Portfolio management. 2. Risk management. 3. Investment analysis.
I. Kopp, P. E., 1944– II. Title.
HG4529.5.C366 2014
332.6–dc23 2014006178

ISBN 978-1-107-00367-5 Hardback
ISBN 978-0-521-17714-6 Paperback

Additional resources for this publication at www.cambridge.org/9781107003675

To Anna, Emily, Staś, Weronika and Helenka

# Contents

# Preface

In this fifth volume of the series 'Mastering Mathematical Finance' we present a self-contained rigorous account of mean-variance portfolio theory, as well as a simple introduction to utility functions and modern risk measures.

Portfolio theory, exploring the optimal allocation of wealth among different assets in an investment portfolio, based on the twin objectives of maximising return while minimising risk, owes its mathematical formulation to the work of Harry Markowitz[1] in 1952; for which he was awarded the Nobel Prize in Economics in 1990. Mean-variance analysis has held sway for more than half a century, and forms part of the core curriculum in financial economics and business studies. In these settings mathematical rigour may suffer at times, and our aim is to provide a carefully motivated treatment of the mathematical background and content of the theory, assuming only basic calculus and linear algebra as prerequisites.

Chapter 1 provides a brief review of the key concepts of return and risk, while noting some defects of variance as a risk measure. Considering a portfolio with only two risky assets, we show in Chapter 2 how the minimum variance portfolio, minimum variance line, market portfolio and capital market line may be found by elementary calculus methods. Chapter 3 contains a careful account of the method of Lagrange multipliers, including a discussion of sufficient conditions for extrema in the special case of quadratic forms. These techniques are applied in Chapter 4 to generalise the formulae obtained for two-asset portfolios to the general case.

The derivation of the Capital Asset Pricing Model (CAPM) follows in Chapter 5, including two proofs of the CAPM formula, based, respectively, on the underlying geometry (to elucidate the role of beta) and linear algebra (leading to the security market line), and introducing performance measures such as the Jensen index and Sharpe ratio. The security characteristic line is shown to aid the least-squares estimation of beta using historical portfolio returns and the market portfolio.

Chapter 6 contains a brief introduction to utility theory. To keep matters simple we restrict to finite sample spaces to discuss preference relations.

---

[1] H. Markowitz, Portfolio selection, *Journal of Finance* 7 (1), (1952), 77–91.

We consider examples of von Neumann–Morgenstern utility functions, link utility maximisation with the No Arbitrage Principle and explain the key role of state price vectors. Finally, we explore the link between utility maximisation and the CAPM and illustrate the role of the certainty equivalent for the risk averse investor.

In the final two chapters the emphasis shifts from variance to measures of downside risk. Chapter 7 contains an account of Value at Risk (VaR), which remains popular in practice despite its well-documented shortcomings. Following a careful look at quantiles and the algebraic properties of VaR, our emphasis is on computing VaR, especially for assets within the Black–Scholes framework. A novel feature is an account of VaR-optimal hedging with put options, which is shown to reduce to a linear programming problem if the parameters are chosen with care.

In Chapter 8 we examine how the defects of VaR can be addressed using coherent risk measures. The principal example discussed is Average Value at Risk (AVaR), which is described in detail, including a careful proof of sub-additivity. AVaR is placed in the context of coherent risk measures, and generalised to yield spectral risk measures. The analysis of hedging with put options in the Black–Scholes setting is revisited, with AVaR in place of VaR, and the outcomes are compared in examples.

Throughout this volume the emphasis is on examples, applications and computations. The underlying theory is presented rigorously, but as simply as possible. Proofs are given in detail, with the more demanding ones left to the end of each chapter to avoid disrupting the flow of ideas. Applications presented in the final chapters make use of background material from the earlier volumes [PF] and [BSM] in the current series. The exercises form an integral part of the volume, and range from simple verification to more challenging problems. Solutions and additional material can be found at www.cambridge.org/9781107003675, which will be updated regularly.

# 1

# Risk and return

Financial investors base their activity on the expectation that their investment will increase over time, leading to an increase in wealth. Over a fixed time period, the investor seeks to maximise the return on the investment, that is, the increase in asset value as a proportion of the initial investment. The final values of most assets (other than loans at a fixed rate of interest) are uncertain, so that the returns on these investments need to be expressed in terms of random variables. To estimate the return on such an asset by a single number it is natural to use the expected value of the return, which averages the returns over all possible outcomes.

Our uncertainty about future market behaviour finds expression in the second key concept in finance: risk. Assets such as stocks, forward contracts and options are risky because we cannot predict their future values with certainty. Assets whose possible final values are more 'widely spread' are naturally seen as entailing greater risk. Thus our initial attempt to measure the riskiness of a random variable will measure the spread of the return, which rational investors will seek to minimise while maximising their return.

In brief, return reflects the efficiency of an investment, risk is concerned with uncertainty. The balance between these two is at the heart of portfolio theory, which seeks to find optimal allocations of the investor's initial wealth among the available assets: maximising return at a given level of risk and minimising risk at a given level of expected return.

## 1.1 Expected return

We are concerned with just two time instants: the present time, denoted by 0, and the future time 1, where 1 may stand for any unit of time. Suppose we make a single-period investment in some stock with the current price $S(0)$ known, and the future price $S(1)$ unknown, hence assumed to be represented by a random variable

$$S(1) : \Omega \rightarrow [0, +\infty),$$

where $\Omega$ is the sample space of some probability space $(\Omega, \mathcal{F}, P)$. The members of $\Omega$ are often called **states** or **scenarios**. (See [PF] for basic definitions.)

When $\Omega$ is finite, $\Omega = \{\omega_1, \ldots, \omega_N\}$, we shall adopt the notation

$$S(1, \omega_i) = S(1)(\omega_i) \quad \text{for } i = 1, \ldots, N,$$

for the possible values of $S(1)$. In this setting it is natural to equip $\Omega$ with the $\sigma$-field $\mathcal{F} = 2^\Omega$ of all its subsets. To define a probability measure $P : \mathcal{F} \rightarrow [0, 1]$ it is sufficient to give its values on single element sets, $P(\{\omega_i\}) = p_i$, by choosing $p_i \in (0, 1]$ such that $\sum_{i=1}^{N} p_i = 1$. We can then compute the expected price at the end of the period

$$\mathbb{E}(S(1)) = \sum_{i=1}^{N} S(1, \omega_i) p_i,$$

and the variance of the price

$$\text{Var}(S(1)) = \sum_{i=1}^{N} (S(1, \omega_i) - \mathbb{E}(S(1)))^2 \, p_i.$$

**Example 1.1**
Assume that $S(0) = 100$ and

$$S(1) = \begin{cases} 120 & \text{with probability } \frac{1}{2}, \\ 90 & \text{with probability } \frac{1}{2}. \end{cases}$$

Then $\mathbb{E}(S(1)) = \frac{1}{2}120 + \frac{1}{2}90 = 105$ and $\text{Var}(S(1)) = (120 - 105)^2 \frac{1}{2} + (90 - 105)^2 \frac{1}{2} = 15^2$. Observe also that the standard deviation, which is the square root of the variance, is equal to $\sqrt{\text{Var}(S(1))} = 15$.

---

**Exercise 1.1** Assume that $U, D \in \mathbb{R}$ are such that $-1 < D < U$. Assume also that $S$ has a binomial distribution, that is

$$P\big(S(1) = S(0)(1 + U)^k (1 + D)^{N-k}\big) = \binom{N}{k} p^k (1 - p)^{N-k},$$

for $k \in \{0, 1, \ldots, N\}$. Compute $\mathbb{E}(S(1))$ and $\mathrm{Var}(S(1))$.

---

When $S(1)$ is continuously distributed, with density function $f : \mathbb{R} \to \mathbb{R}$, then

$$\mathbb{E}(S(1)) = \int_{-\infty}^{\infty} x f(x) dx,$$

and

$$\mathrm{Var}(S(1)) = \int_{-\infty}^{\infty} (x - \mathbb{E}(S(1)))^2 f(x) dx.$$

**Example 1.2**
Assume that $S(1) = S(0) \exp(m + sZ)$, where $Z$ is a random variable with standard normal distribution $N(0, 1)$. This means that $S(1)$ has lognormal distribution. The density function of $S(1)$ is equal to

$$f(x) = \frac{1}{xs\sqrt{2\pi}} e^{-\frac{\left(\ln \frac{x}{S(0)} - m\right)^2}{2s^2}} \quad \text{for } x > 0,$$

and 0 for $x \leq 0$. We can compute the expected price as

$$\mathbb{E}(S(1)) = \int_0^{\infty} x f(x) dx$$

$$= \int_0^{\infty} \frac{1}{s\sqrt{2\pi}} e^{-\frac{\left(\ln \frac{x}{S(0)} - m\right)^2}{2s^2}} dx$$

$$= \int_{-\infty}^{\infty} S(0) e^{sy+m} \frac{1}{\sqrt{2\pi}} e^{-\frac{y^2}{2}} dy \quad (\text{taking } y = \frac{1}{s}\left(\ln \frac{x}{S(0)} - m\right))$$

$$= S(0) e^{m + \frac{s^2}{2}} \int_{-\infty}^{\infty} \frac{1}{\sqrt{2\pi}} e^{-\frac{(y-s)^2}{2}} dy$$

$$= S(0) e^{m + \frac{s^2}{2}}.$$

**Exercise 1.2**  Consider $S(1)$ from Example 1.2. Show that
$$\text{Var}(S(1)) = S(0)^2 \left(e^{s^2} - 1\right) e^{2m+s^2}.$$

While we may allow any probability space, we must make sure that negative values of the random variable $S(1)$ are excluded since negative prices make no sense from the point of view of economics. This means that the distribution of $S(1)$ has to be supported on $[0, +\infty)$ (meaning that $P(S(1) \geq 0) = 1$).

The **return** (also called the rate of return) on the investment $S$ is a random variable $K : \Omega \to \mathbb{R}$, defined as
$$K = \frac{S(1) - S(0)}{S(0)}.$$

By the linearity of mathematical expectation, the **expected** (or mean) **return** is given by
$$\mathbb{E}(K) = \frac{\mathbb{E}(S(1)) - S(0)}{S(0)}.$$

We introduce the convention of using the Greek letter $\mu$ for expectations of various random returns
$$\mu = \mathbb{E}(K),$$

with various subscripts indicating the context, if necessary.

The relationships between the prices and returns can be written as
$$S(1) = S(0)(1 + K),$$
$$\mathbb{E}(S(1)) = S(0)(1 + \mu),$$

which illustrates the possibility of reversing the approach: given the returns we can find the prices.

The requirement that $S(1)$ is nonnegative implies that we must have $K \geq -1$. This in particular excludes the possibility of considering $K$ with Gaussian (normal) distribution.

At time 1 a dividend may be paid. In practice, after the dividend is paid, the stock price drops by this amount, which is logical. Thus we have to determine the price that includes the dividend; more precisely, we must distinguish between the right to receive that price (the cum dividend price) and the price after the dividend is paid (the ex dividend price). We assume that $S(1)$ denotes the latter, hence the definition of the return has to be modified to account for dividends:

$$K = \frac{S(1) + \text{Div}(1) - S(0)}{S(0)}.$$

A **bond** is a special security that pays a certain sum of money, known in advance, at maturity; this sum is the same in each state. The return on a bond is not random (recall that we are dealing with a single time period). Consider a bond paying a unit of home currency at time 1, that is $B(1) = 1$, which is purchased for $B(0) < 1$. Then

$$R = \frac{1 - B(0)}{B(0)}$$

defines the **risk-free return**. The bond price can be expressed as

$$B(0) = \frac{1}{1 + R},$$

giving the present value of a unit at time 1.

---

**Exercise 1.3**  Compute the expected returns for the stocks described in Exercise 1.1 and Example 1.2.

---

**Exercise 1.4**  Assume that $S(0) = 80$ and that the ex dividend price is

$$S(1) = \begin{cases} 60 & \text{with probability } \frac{1}{6}, \\ 80 & \text{with probability } \frac{3}{6}, \\ 90 & \text{with probability } \frac{2}{6}. \end{cases}$$

The company will pay out a constant dividend (independent of the future stock price). Compute the dividend for which the expected return on stock would be 20%.

---

## 1.2 Variance as a risk measure

The concept of risk in finance is captured in many ways. The basic and most widely used one is concerned with risk as uncertainty of the unknown future value of some quantity in question (here we are concerned with return). This uncertainty is understood as the scatter around some reference point. A natural candidate for the reference value is the mathematical expectation (though other benchmarks are sometimes considered). The extent of scatter is conveniently measured by the variance. This notion takes care of two aspects of risk:

    (i) The distances between possible values and the expectation.

    (ii) The probabilities of attaining the various possible values.

**Definition 1.3**

By (the measure of) risk we mean the **variance** of the return

$$\text{Var}(K) = \mathbb{E}(K - \mu)^2 = \mathbb{E}(K^2) - \mu^2,$$

or the **standard deviation** $\sqrt{\text{Var}(K)}$.

The variance of the return can be computed from the variance of $S(1)$,

$$\text{Var}(K) = \text{Var}\left(\frac{S(1) - S(0)}{S(0)}\right)$$

$$= \frac{1}{S(0)^2}\text{Var}(S(1) - S(0))$$

$$= \frac{1}{S(0)^2}\text{Var}(S(1)).$$

We use the Greek letter $\sigma$ for standard deviations of various random returns

$$\sigma = \sqrt{\text{Var}(K)},$$

qualified by subscripts, as required.

---

**Exercise 1.5** In a market with risk-free return $R > 0$, we buy a 'leveraged' stock $S$ at time 0 with a mixture of cash and a loan at rate $R$. To buy the stock for $S(0)$ we use $wS(0)$ of our own cash and borrow $(1 - w)S(0)$, for some $w \in (0, 1)$. Denote the returns at time 1 on the stock and leveraged position by $K_S$ and $K_{\text{lev}}$ respectively.

Derive the relation

$$K_{\text{lev}} = R + \frac{1}{w}(K_S - R),$$

and find the relationship between the standard deviations of the stock and the leveraged position.

Standard deviation alone does not fully capture the risk of an investment. We illustrate this with a simple example.

**Example 1.4**

Consider three assets with today's prices $S_i(0) = 100$ for $i = 1, 2, 3$ and time 1 prices with the following distributions:

$$S_1(1) = \begin{cases} 120 & \text{with probability } \frac{1}{2}, \\ 90 & \text{with probability } \frac{1}{2}, \end{cases}$$

$$S_2(1) = \begin{cases} 140 & \text{with probability } \frac{1}{2}, \\ 90 & \text{with probability } \frac{1}{2}, \end{cases}$$

$$S_3(1) = \begin{cases} 130 & \text{with probability } \frac{1}{2}, \\ 100 & \text{with probability } \frac{1}{2}. \end{cases}$$

We can see that

$$\sigma_1 = \sqrt{\text{Var}(K_1)} = 0.15,$$
$$\sigma_2 = \sqrt{\text{Var}(K_2)} = 0.25,$$
$$\sigma_3 = \sqrt{\text{Var}(K_2)} = 0.15.$$

Here $\sigma_2 > \sigma_1$ and $\sigma_3 = \sigma_1$, but both the second and third assets are preferable to the first, since at time 1 they bring in more cash. We shall return to this example in the next section.

When considering the risk of an investment we should take into account both the expectation and and the standard deviation of the return. Given the choice between two securities a rational investor will, if possible, choose that with the higher expected return and lower standard deviation, that is, lower risk. This motivates the following definition.

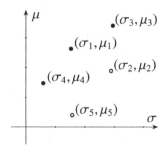

**Figure 1.1** Efficient subset.

**Definition 1.5**

We say that a security with expected return $\mu_1$ and standard deviation $\sigma_1$ **dominates** another security with expected return $\mu_2$ and standard deviation $\sigma_2$ whenever

$$\mu_1 \geq \mu_2 \quad \text{and} \quad \sigma_1 \leq \sigma_2.$$

The meaning of the word 'dominates' is that we assume the investors to be risk averse. One can imagine an investor whose personal goal is just the excitement of playing the market. This person will not pay any attention to return or may prefer higher risk. However, it is not our intention to cover such individuals by our theory.

The playground for portfolio theory will be the $(\sigma, \mu)$-plane, in fact the right half-plane since the standard deviation is non-negative. Each security is represented by a dot on this plane. This means that we are making a simplification by assuming that the expectation and variance are all that matters when investment decisions are made.

We assume that the dominating securities are preferred, which geometrically (geographically) means that for any two securities, the one lying further north-west in the $(\sigma, \mu)$-plane is preferable. This ordering does not allow us to compare all pairs: in Figure 1.1 we see for instance that the pairs $(\sigma_1, \mu_1)$ and $(\sigma_3, \mu_3)$ are not comparable.

Given a set $A$ of securities in the $(\sigma, \mu)$-plane, we consider the subset of all maximal elements with respect to the dominance relation and call it the **efficient subset**. If the set $A$ is finite, finding the efficient subsets reduces to eliminating the dominated securities. Figure 1.1 shows a set of five securities with efficient subset consisting of just three, numbered 1, 3 and 4.

---

**Exercise 1.6**   Assume that we have three assets. The first has expected return $\mu_1 = 10\%$ and standard deviation of return equal to $\sigma_1 = 0.25$. The second has expected return $\mu_2 = 15\%$ and standard deviation of return equal to $\sigma_2 = 0.3$. Assume that the future prices of the third asset will have $\mathbb{E}(S_3(1)) = 100$, $\sqrt{Var(S_3(1))} = 20$. Find the ranges of prices $S_3(0)$ so that the following conditions are satisfied:

  (i)  The third asset dominates the first asset.

 (ii)  The third asset dominates the second asset.

(iii)  No asset is dominated by another asset.

---

## 1.3   Semi-variance

Consider the three assets described in Example 1.4. Although $\sigma_1 = \sigma_3$, the third asset carries no 'downside risk', since neither outcome for $S_3(1)$ involves a loss for the investor. Similarly, although $\sigma_2 > \sigma_1$, the downside risk for the second asset is the same as that for the first (a 50% chance of incurring a loss of 10), but the expected return for the second asset is 15%, making it the more attractive investment even though, as measured by variance, it is more risky. Since investors regard risk as concerned with failure (i.e. downside risk), the following modification of variance is sometimes used. It is called **semi-variance** and is computed by a formula that takes into account only the unfavourable outcomes, where the return is below the expected value

$$\mathbb{E}(\min\{0, K - \mu\})^2. \tag{1.1}$$

The square root of semi-variance is denoted by semi-$\sigma$. However, this notion still does not agree fully with the intuition.

**Example 1.6**

Assume that $\Omega = \{\omega_1, \omega_2\}$, $P(\{\omega_1\}) = P(\{\omega_2\}) = \frac{1}{2}$ and

$$K(\omega_1) = 10\%,$$
$$K(\omega_2) = 20\%.$$

Consider a modification $K'$ with

$$K'(\omega_1) = 10\%,$$
$$K'(\omega_2) = 30\%.$$

Then $K'$ is definitely better than $K$ but the semi-variance and the variance for $K'$ are both higher than for $K$.

If variance or semi-variance are to represent risk, it is illogical that a better version should be regarded as more risky. This defect can be rectified by replacing the expectation by some other reference point, for instance the risk-free return with the following modification of (1.1),

$$\mathbb{E}(\min\{0, K - R\})^2,$$

which eliminates the above unwanted feature. Instead of the risk-free rate, one can also consider the return required by the investor.

These versions are not very popular in the financial world, the variance being the basic measure of risk. In our presentation of portfolio theory we follow the historical tradition and take variance as the measure of risk. It is possible to develop a version of the theory for alternative ways of measuring risk. In most cases, however, such theories do not produce neat analytic formulae as is the case for the mean and variance.

We will return to a more general discussion of risk measures in the final chapters of this volume. An analysis of the popular concept of Value at Risk (VaR), which has been used extensively in the banking and investment sectors since the 1990s, will lead us to conclude that, despite its ubiquity, this risk measure has serious shortcomings, especially when dealing with mixed distributions. We will then examine an alternative which remedies these defects but still remains mathematically tractable.

# 2

# Portfolios consisting of two assets

We begin our discussion of portfolio risk and expected return with portfolios consisting of just two securities. This has the advantage that the key concepts of mean-variance portfolio theory can be expressed in simple geometric terms.

For a given allocation of resources between the two assets comprising the portfolio, the mean and variance of the return on the entire portfolio are expressed in terms of the means and variances of, and (crucially) the covariance between, the returns on the individual assets. This enables us to examine the set of all feasible weightings of (in other words, allocations of funds to) the different assets in the portfolio, and to find the unique weighting with minimum variance. We also find the collection of efficient portfolios – ones that are not dominated by any other. Finally, adding a risk-free asset, we find the so-called market portfolio, which is the unique portfolio providing an optimal combination with the risk-free asset.

We denote the prices of the securities as $S_1(t)$ and $S_2(t)$ for $t = 0, 1$. We start with a motivating example.

**Example 2.1**
Let $\Omega = \{\omega_1, \omega_2\}$, $S_1(0) = 200$, $S_2(0) = 300$. Assume that

$$P(\{\omega_1\}) = P(\{\omega_1\}) = \frac{1}{2},$$

and that

$$S_1(1, \omega_1) = 260, \qquad S_2(1, \omega_1) = 270,$$
$$S_1(1, \omega_2) = 180, \qquad S_2(1, \omega_2) = 360.$$

The expected returns and standard deviations for the two assets are

$$\mu_1 = 10\%, \qquad \mu_2 = 5\%,$$
$$\sigma_1 = 20\%, \qquad \sigma_2 = 15\%.$$

Assume that we spend $V(0) = 500$, buying a single share of stock $S_1$ and a single share of stock $S_2$. At time 1 we will have

$$V(1, \omega_1) = 260 + 270 = 530,$$
$$V(1, \omega_2) = 180 + 360 = 540.$$

The expected return on the investment is 7% and the standard deviation is just 1%. We can see that by diversifying the investment into two stocks we have considerably reduced the risk.

## 2.1  Return

From the above example we see that the risk can be reduced by diversification. In this section we discuss how to minimise risk when investing in two stocks.

Suppose that we buy $x_1$ shares of stock $S_1$ and $x_2$ shares of stock $S_2$. The **initial value** of this portfolio is

$$V_{(x_1, x_2)}(0) = x_1 S_1(0) + x_2 S_2(0).$$

When we design a portfolio, usually its initial value is the starting point of our considerations and it is given. The decision on the number of shares in each asset will follow from the decision on the division of our wealth, which is our primary concern and is expressed by means of the **weights** defined by

$$w_1 = \frac{x_1 S_1(0)}{V_{(x_1,x_2)}(0)}, \quad w_2 = \frac{x_2 S_2(0)}{V_{(x_1,x_2)}(0)}. \tag{2.1}$$

If the initial wealth $V(0)$ and the weights $w_1, w_2, w_1+w_2 = 1$, are given, then the funds allocated to a particular stock are $w_1 V(0)$, $w_2 V(0)$, respectively, and the numbers of shares we buy are

$$x_1 = \frac{w_1 V(0)}{S_1(0)}, \quad x_2 = \frac{w_2 V(0)}{S_2(0)}.$$

At the end of the period the securities prices change, which gives the final value of the portfolio as a random variable

$$V_{(x_1,x_2)}(1) = x_1 S_1(1) + x_2 S_2(1).$$

To express the return on a portfolio we employ the weights rather than the numbers of shares since this is more convenient.

The return on the investment in two assets depends on the method of allocation of the funds (the weights) and the corresponding returns. The vector of weights will be denoted by $\mathbf{w} = (w_1, w_2)$, or in matrix notation

$$\mathbf{w} = \begin{bmatrix} w_1 \\ w_2 \end{bmatrix},$$

and the return of the corresponding portfolio by $K_{\mathbf{w}}$.

**Proposition 2.2**
*The return $K_{\mathbf{w}}$ on a portfolio consisting of two securities is the weighted average*

$$K_{\mathbf{w}} = w_1 K_1 + w_2 K_2, \tag{2.2}$$

*where $w_1$ and $w_2$ are the weights and $K_1$ and $K_2$ the returns on the two components.*

*Proof* With the numbers of shares computed as above, we have the following formula for the value of the portfolio

$$
\begin{aligned}
V_{(x_1,x_2)}(1) &= x_1 S_1(1) + x_2 S_2(1) \\
&= \frac{w_1 V_{(x_1,x_2)}(0)}{S_1(0)} S_1(0)(1 + K_1) + \frac{w_2 V_{(x_1,x_2)}(0)}{S_2(0)} S_2(0)(1 + K_2) \\
&= V_{(x_1,x_2)}(0) \left( w_1(1 + K_1) + w_2(1 + K_2) \right) \\
&= V_{(x_1,x_2)}(0)(1 + w_1 K_1 + w_2 K_2), \qquad \text{(since } w_1 + w_2 = 1\text{)}
\end{aligned}
$$

hence

$$K_{\mathbf{w}} = \frac{V_{(x_1,x_2)}(1) - V_{(x_1,x_2)}(0)}{V_{(x_1,x_2)}(0)} = w_1 K_1 + w_2 K_2.$$

□

In reality, the numbers of shares have to be integers. This, however, puts a constraint on possible weights since not all percentage splits of our wealth can be realised. To simplify matters we make the assumption that our stock position, that is, the number of shares, can be any real number.

When the number of shares of given stock is positive, then we say that we have a long position in the stock. We shall assume that we can also hold a negative number of shares of stock. This is known as **short-selling**. Short-selling is a mechanism by which we borrow stock at time 0 and sell it immediately; we then need to buy it back at time 1 to return it to the lender. This mechanism gives us additional money at time 0 that can be invested in a different security.

**Example 2.3**
Consider the stocks $S_1$ and $S_2$ from Example 2.1. Suppose that at time 0 we have $V(0) = 600$. Suppose also that at time 0 we borrow three shares of stock $S_1$, meaning that we choose $x_1 = -3$. We sell the three shares of stock, which together with $V(0)$ gives us $3 \cdot 200 + 600 = 1200$ to invest in the second asset. We can thus take $x_2 = 4$. Note that

$$V_{(x_1,x_2)}(0) = x_1 S_1(0) + x_2 S_2(0) = 600 = V(0).$$

At time 1 we have the proceeds from holding four shares of $S_2$, but we need to buy back the three shares of $S_1$ at its market value. Since

$$V_{(x_1,x_2)}(1) = x_1 S_1(1) + x_2 S_2(1),$$

we see that

$$V_{(x_1,x_2)}(1, \omega_1) = -3 \cdot 260 + 4 \cdot 270 = 300,$$
$$V_{(x_1,x_2)}(1, \omega_2) = -3 \cdot 180 + 4 \cdot 360 = 900.$$

We can compute the weights using (2.1)

$$w_1 = \frac{-3 \cdot 200}{600} = -1, \quad w_2 = \frac{4 \cdot 300}{600} = 2.$$

We see that, as expected, $w_1 + w_2 = 1$.

**Exercise 2.1** Compute the expected return and the standard deviation of the return for the investment from Example 2.3. Explain why this portfolio is less desirable than investing in any of the two securities.

When short-selling is allowed, we assume that the weights can be any real numbers whose sum is one. For example, if at time 0 we take a short position in stock $S_1$, then $x_1$ and hence the weight $w_1$ is negative, and we need $w_2$ to be larger than 1, so that $w_1 + w_2 = 1$.

In real markets short-selling comes with restrictions. To take a short position a trader usually needs to pay a lending fee or to make a deposit. Throughout the discussion we make the simplifying assumption that short-selling is free of such charges. Since not all real markets allow short-selling, we shall sometimes distinguish special cases where all the weights are non-negative.

## 2.2 Attainable set

Finding the risk of a portfolio requires, apart from the risks of the components and the weights, some knowledge about their statistical relationship. Recall from [PF] the notion of covariance of two random variables, $X, Y$:

$$\text{Cov}(X, Y) = \mathbb{E}\left[(X - \mathbb{E}(X))(Y - \mathbb{E}(Y))\right] = \mathbb{E}(XY) - \mathbb{E}(X)\mathbb{E}(Y), \qquad (2.3)$$

with $\text{Cov}(X, X) = \text{Var}(X) = \sigma_X^2$ in particular. Applying the Schwarz inequality ([PF, Lemma 3.49]) to $X - \mathbb{E}(X)$ and $Y - \mathbb{E}(Y)$ we obtain

$$|\text{Cov}(X, Y)| \leq \sigma_X \sigma_Y. \qquad (2.4)$$

This leads immediately to an inequality, that we leave as an exercise.

**Exercise 2.2** Suppose that random variables $X, Y$ have finite variances. Show that $\sigma_{X+Y} \leq \sigma_X + \sigma_Y$.

Let us introduce the following notation for the **covariance** of the returns on the stocks $S_1, S_2$ :

$$\sigma_{ij} = \text{Cov}(K_i, K_j),$$

for $i, j = 1, 2$. In particular,

$$\sigma_{11} = \text{Cov}(K_1, K_1) = \text{Var}(K_1) = \sigma_1^2,$$
$$\sigma_{22} = \text{Cov}(K_2, K_2) = \text{Var}(K_2) = \sigma_2^2.$$

From (2.3) we see that

$$\sigma_{12} = \sigma_{21}.$$

If the returns are independent, then we have $\sigma_{12} = 0$.

For convenience, the so-called **correlation coefficient** is also introduced

$$\rho_{ij} = \frac{\sigma_{ij}}{\sigma_i \sigma_j}. \tag{2.5}$$

For this to make sense we have to assume that the variances of both returns are non-zero. The variance is zero in one case only, namely when the random variable is constant (almost surely). So we assume that the returns on stocks are genuine, non-constant, random variables, unlike bonds, where the return is the same in each state (scenario).

By (2.4) the correlation coefficient satisfies

$$-1 \leq \rho_{ij} \leq 1.$$

This makes correlation a good coefficient to measure dependence. If the correlation coefficient is close to 1 or $-1$, then there is a strong influence of one variable on the other. It is more difficult to make such assertions by looking at covariance alone.

**Theorem 2.4**

*The expected return and the variance of the return on a portfolio are given by*

$$\mu_{\mathbf{w}} = \mathbb{E}(K_{\mathbf{w}}) = w_1 \mu_1 + w_2 \mu_2, \tag{2.6}$$
$$\sigma_{\mathbf{w}}^2 = \text{Var}(K_{\mathbf{w}}) = w_1^2 \sigma_1^2 + w_2^2 \sigma_2^2 + 2 w_1 w_2 \sigma_{12}. \tag{2.7}$$

*Proof* Equality (2.6) follows directly from (2.2) and linearity of mathematical expectation:

$$\mu_{\mathbf{w}} = \mathbb{E}(K_{\mathbf{w}}) = \mathbb{E}(w_1 K_1 + w_2 K_2) = w_1 \mathbb{E}(K_1) + w_2 \mathbb{E}(K_2).$$

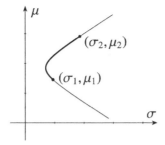

**Figure 2.1** Attainable set.

We wish to compute the standard deviation of the return on a portfolio of two stocks:

$$\sigma_{\mathbf{w}}^2 = \mathbb{E}(K_{\mathbf{w}}^2) - \mu_{\mathbf{w}}^2.$$

Substituting (2.2) and (2.6), and using (2.3) in the last equality, gives

$$\begin{aligned}
\sigma_{\mathbf{w}}^2 &= \mathbb{E}(w_1^2 K_1^2 + w_2^2 K_2^2 + 2w_1 w_2 K_1 K_2) - w_1^2 \mu_1^2 - w_2^2 \mu_2^2 - 2w_1 w_2 \mu_1 \mu_2 \\
&= w_1^2[\mathbb{E}(K_1^2) - \mu_1^2] + w_2^2[\mathbb{E}(K_2^2) - \mu_2^2] + 2w_1 w_2[\mathbb{E}(K_1 K_2) - \mu_1 \mu_2] \\
&= w_1^2 \sigma_1^2 + w_2^2 \sigma_2^2 + 2w_1 w_2 \sigma_{12},
\end{aligned}$$

which concludes the proof.                                                    □

**Corollary 2.5**
*Using (2.5) we can rewrite the formula for the variance of a portfolio as*

$$\sigma_{\mathbf{w}}^2 = w_1^2 \sigma_1^2 + w_2^2 \sigma_2^2 + 2w_1 w_2 \rho_{12} \sigma_1 \sigma_2. \tag{2.8}$$

**Corollary 2.6**
*Using the following matrix notation*

$$\mathbf{w} = \begin{bmatrix} w_1 \\ w_2 \end{bmatrix}, \quad \boldsymbol{\mu} = \begin{bmatrix} \mu_1 \\ \mu_2 \end{bmatrix},$$

$$C = \begin{bmatrix} \sigma_1^2 & \sigma_{12} \\ \sigma_{12} & \sigma_2^2 \end{bmatrix},$$

*equations (2.6)–(2.7) can be written as*

$$\mu_{\mathbf{w}} = \mathbf{w}^{\mathrm{T}} \boldsymbol{\mu}, \tag{2.9}$$

$$\sigma_{\mathbf{w}}^2 = \mathbf{w}^{\mathrm{T}} C \mathbf{w} \tag{2.10}$$

*where we denote the transpose of the matrix A by $A^{\mathrm{T}}$.*

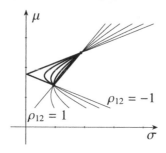

**Figure 2.2** Portfolio lines for various values of $\rho_{12}$.

The collection of all portfolios that can be manufactured by means of two given assets (in other words, the **attainable set**, also known as the feasible set) can conveniently be depicted in the $(\sigma, \mu)$-plane. Assume that $\mu_1 \neq \mu_2$ (let $\mu_1 < \mu_2$ for instance). Take the first weight as a parameter, writing $w = w_1$. Hence $w_2 = 1 - w$, $\mathbf{w} = (w, 1 - w)$ and the expected return and standard deviation of the portfolio as functions of $w$ have the form

$$\mu_{\mathbf{w}} = w\mu_1 + (1 - w)\mu_2, \tag{2.11}$$
$$\sigma_{\mathbf{w}}^2 = w^2\sigma_1^2 + (1 - w)^2\sigma_2^2 + 2w(1 - w)\rho_{12}\sigma_1\sigma_2.$$

The attainable set is therefore a curve parameterised by $w$. An example of such set is depicted in Figure 2.1. If short-selling is not allowed we restrict our attention to the segment corresponding to $w \in [0, 1]$. This is the thicker part of the curve in Figure 2.1.

The shape of the line depends on the correlation coefficient $\rho_{12}$. This is shown in Figure 2.2. We see that for negative $\rho_{12}$ we can reduce the risk of the portfolio, at the same time achieving an expected return between the expected returns of the two risky assets.

Suppose that the position of the two basis securities is such as in Figure 2.3, namely one dominates the other. The portfolios manufactured using the securities may give the investor extra choice. For instance we may obtain the portfolios whose risk is lower than the risk of any of the individual assets, or portfolios with expected return higher than any of components. This shows that rejecting the dominated security would be a bad decision.

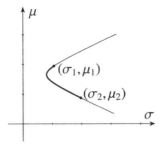

**Figure 2.3** Portfolio line with one asset dominating the other.

---

**Exercise 2.3** Assume that $\mu_1 = 10\%$, $\mu_2 = 20\%$, $\sigma_1 = 0.1$, $\sigma_2 = 0.3$ and $\rho_{12} = 0.7$. Find a portfolio for which $\sigma_w < \sigma_1$. Is it possible to construct a portfolio with expected return equal to 30%?

---

From (2.11) we see that $\mu_w$ is affine, and $\sigma_w^2$ is a quadratic function with respect to $w$. Since a graph of the root of a quadratic function is a hyperbola, one can guess that the attainable set consisting of all points $(\mu_w, \sigma_w)$ should be a hyperbola.

**Theorem 2.7**
*If $\mu_1 \neq \mu_2$ and $\rho_{12} \in (-1, 1)$, then the attainable set is a hyperbola with its centre on the vertical axis.*

*Proof* See page 31. ☐

---

**Exercise 2.4** What is the shape of the attainable set when $\mu_1 = \mu_2$?

---

We shall return to the above discussion when working with $n$ assets later on. It may come as a surprise that from the point of view of technical difficulties, the general case will be as simple as the particular situation just worked out, where only two assets are involved. It will also turn out that the case of many assets reduces to the case of just two and we will be able to draw valuable conclusions, that remain valid in general case, from the discussion of the present chapter.

In practice we can reject some of the portfolios drawing on the basic preference property, namely, given two portfolios with the same risk, the

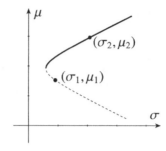

**Figure 2.4** Efficient frontier.

one with higher expected return is preferable. So we may discard the lower part of the curve restricting our attention to the upper, called the efficient set or frontier, as shown in Figure 2.4. More precisely, a portfolio is called **efficient** if there is no other portfolio, except itself, that dominates it. The set of efficient portfolios among all attainable portfolios is called the **efficient frontier**.

## 2.3  Special cases

Our first special case is when $\rho_{12} = -1$. From (2.8),

$$\sigma_{\mathbf{w}}^2 = w_1^2 \sigma_1^2 + w_2^2 \sigma_2^2 - 2w_1 w_2 \sigma_1 \sigma_2$$
$$= (w_1 \sigma_1 - w_2 \sigma_2)^2,$$

hence

$$\sigma_{\mathbf{w}} = |w_1 \sigma_1 - w_2 \sigma_2|.$$

Since $\sigma_{\mathbf{w}}$ is non-negative the smallest value it could take is $\sigma_{\mathbf{w}} = 0$. Taking $w_1 = w$ and $w_2 = 1 - w$ gives

$$\sigma_{\mathbf{w}} = |w\sigma_1 - (1 - w)\sigma_2|, \qquad (2.12)$$

and we can solve for $\sigma_{\mathbf{w}} = 0$, obtaining

$$w = \frac{\sigma_2}{\sigma_1 + \sigma_2}, \qquad 1 - w = \frac{\sigma_1}{\sigma_1 + \sigma_2}. \qquad (2.13)$$

Since $\sigma_1, \sigma_2 \geq 0$, we can see that $w \in [0, 1]$, hence we can minimise our risk to zero without short-selling.

From (2.12) and (2.11) one can show that the attainable set consists of two half lines, emanating from the vertical axis (see Figure 2.5).

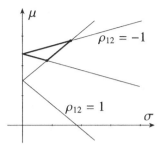

**Figure 2.5** Attainable set for $\rho_{12} = \pm 1$.

---

**Exercise 2.5**   Assuming that $\rho_{12} = -1$, derive the formulae for the half lines that form the attainable set.

---

Our second case is $\rho_{12} = 1$. Then

$$\sigma_{\mathbf{w}}^2 = w_1^2 \sigma_1^2 + w_2^2 \sigma_2^2 + 2w_1 w_2 \sigma_1 \sigma_2$$
$$= (w_1 \sigma_1 + w_2 \sigma_2)^2,$$

and

$$\sigma_{\mathbf{w}} = |w_1 \sigma_1 + w_2 \sigma_2|.$$

Similarly to the previous case, we obtain $\sigma_{\mathbf{w}} = 0$ for

$$w_1 = \frac{-\sigma_2}{\sigma_1 - \sigma_2}, \qquad w_2 = \frac{\sigma_1}{\sigma_1 - \sigma_2}. \qquad (2.14)$$

This requires that $\sigma_1 \neq \sigma_2$, and we exclude this trivial case. Since $\sigma_1, \sigma_2 \geq 0$, either $w$ or $1 - w$ has to be negative, hence we can not minimise risk to zero without short-selling. Without short-selling the smallest risk is either at $w = 0$ or at $w = 1$.

---

**Exercise 2.6**   Assuming that $\rho_{12} = 1$ and $\sigma_1 \neq \sigma_2$, derive the formulae for the half lines that form the feasible set.

---

**Exercise 2.7**   Investigate what happens when $\rho_{12} = 1$ and $\sigma_1 = \sigma_2$.

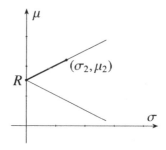

**Figure 2.6** Portfolio line for one risky and one risk-free security.

---

**Exercise 2.8**   Investigate what happens when illegal data with $|\rho_{12}| > 1$ are considered.

---

Finally, consider a particular case where one of the assets is **risk-free**, $\sigma_1 = 0$, say. The return on this asset is sure, $\mu_1 = R$ and a reasonable assumption is that $R < \mu_2$ since otherwise risk-averse investors would never invest in the risky asset, its price should fall and so the expected return should grow above the risk-free level. (The preferences of investors will be discussed in more detail later.) The return and risk for portfolios take a simplified form

$$\mu_{\mathbf{w}} = w_1 R + w_2 \mu_2,$$
$$\sigma_{\mathbf{w}}^2 = w_2^2 \sigma_2^2$$

giving

$$\sigma_{\mathbf{w}} = |w_2| \sigma_2,$$

and so the set in the $(\sigma, \mu)$-plane is as shown in Figure 2.6 (with redundant lower part according to the preference relation).

The segment between the risk-free asset and the asset characterised by $(\sigma_2, \mu_2)$ corresponds to positive weights. The line above $(\sigma_2, \mu_2)$ requires taking a short position in the risk-free asset, in other words, borrowing at the risk-free rate (which we assume here to be possible). The rejected lower segment shows portfolios with a short position in the risky asset.

## 2.4 Minimum variance portfolio

We return to the case of two risky securities, $S_1$ and $S_2$. We wish to minimise the variance $\sigma_{\mathbf{w}}^2$ – or, equivalently, the standard deviation $\sigma_{\mathbf{w}}$. We start with a theorem where the problem is solved when there are no restrictions on short-selling.

**Theorem 2.8**
*If short-selling is allowed, then the portfolio with minimum variance has the weights* $\mathbf{w}_{\min} = (w_1, w_2)$ *with*

$$w_1 = \frac{a}{a+b}, \qquad w_2 = \frac{b}{a+b},$$

*where*

$$a = \sigma_2^2 - \rho_{12}\sigma_1\sigma_2,$$
$$b = \sigma_1^2 - \rho_{12}\sigma_1\sigma_2,$$

*unless both* $\rho_{12} = 1$ *and* $\sigma_1 = \sigma_2$.

*Proof*   When $\rho_{12} = -1$, then from (2.13)

$$w_1 = \frac{\sigma_2}{\sigma_1 + \sigma_2} = \frac{\sigma_2(\sigma_1 + \sigma_2)}{(\sigma_1 + \sigma_2)^2} = \frac{a}{a+b}.$$

Similarly, for $\rho_{12} = 1$, using (2.14)

$$w_1 = \frac{-\sigma_2}{\sigma_1 - \sigma_2} = \frac{-\sigma_2(\sigma_1 - \sigma_2)}{(\sigma_1 - \sigma_2)^2} = \frac{a}{a+b}.$$

When $\rho_{12} \in (-1, 1)$,

$$\sigma_{\mathbf{w}}^2 = w^2\sigma_1^2 + (1-w)^2\sigma_2^2 + 2w(1-w)\rho_{12}\sigma_1\sigma_2$$

is a quadratic function. We compute the derivative of $\sigma_{\mathbf{w}}^2$ with respect to $w$ and equate it to 0:

$$2w\sigma_1^2 - 2(1-w)\sigma_2^2 + 2(1-w)\rho_{12}\sigma_1\sigma_2 - 2w\rho_{12}\sigma_1\sigma_2 = 0.$$

Solving for $w$ gives the above result. The second derivative is positive,

$$2\sigma_1^2 + 2\sigma_2^2 - 4\rho_{12}\sigma_1\sigma_2 > 2\sigma_1^2 + 2\sigma_2^2 - 4\sigma_1\sigma_2 = 2(\sigma_1 - \sigma_2)^2 \geq 0,$$

which shows that we have a global minimum.   □

**Exercise 2.9**   For which $\rho_{12}$ will $\mathbf{w}_{\min}$ require short-selling?

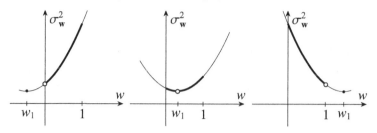

**Figure 2.7** Smallest variance with short-selling restrictions.

In Corollary 2.6 the return and variance of a given portfolio were stated in terms of the covariance matrix

$$C = \begin{bmatrix} \sigma_1^2 & \sigma_{12} \\ \sigma_{12} & \sigma_2^2 \end{bmatrix}$$

for the two assets. We now do the same for the weights of the minimum variance portfolio.

Since $S_1$ and $S_2$ are risky assets, the matrix $C$ is invertible. By Cramer's rule

$$C^{-1} = \frac{1}{\det C} \begin{bmatrix} \sigma_2^2 & -\sigma_{12} \\ -\sigma_{12} & \sigma_1^2 \end{bmatrix}.$$

So we have, writing $\mathbf{1} = (1, 1)$,

$$C^{-1}\mathbf{1} = \frac{1}{\det C} \begin{bmatrix} \sigma_2^2 - \sigma_{12} \\ \sigma_1^2 - \sigma_{12} \end{bmatrix} = \frac{1}{\det C} \begin{bmatrix} a \\ b \end{bmatrix},$$

$$\mathbf{1}^{\mathrm{T}} C^{-1} \mathbf{1} = \frac{1}{\det C}(\sigma_1^2 + \sigma_2^2 - 2\sigma_{12}) = \frac{1}{\det C}(a + b),$$

since $\sigma_{12} = \rho_{12}\sigma_1\sigma_2$. We have proved the following:

**Corollary 2.9**

*The vector* $\mathbf{w}_{\min} = (w_1, w_2)$ *of weights of the minimum variance portfolio found in Theorem 2.8 has the form*

$$\mathbf{w}_{\min} = \frac{C^{-1}\mathbf{1}}{\mathbf{1}^{\mathrm{T}} C^{-1} \mathbf{1}}.$$

We now discuss what happens when short-selling is not allowed. We need to find the minimum of

$$\sigma_{\mathbf{w}}^2 = w^2\sigma_1^2 + (1 - w)^2\sigma_2^2 + 2w(1 - w)\rho_{12}\sigma_1\sigma_2$$

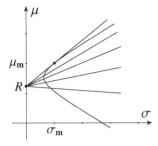

**Figure 2.8** Feasible set after adding a risk-free security.

for restricted values of the weight $0 \leq w \leq 1$. Let $w_1$ be the coefficient from Theorem 2.8. The claim is illustrated in Figure 2.7, where the bold parts correspond to portfolios with no short-selling. We can see that the smallest variance is attained at $\mathbf{w}_{min} = (w, 1 - w)$ with

$$w = \begin{cases} 0 & \text{if } w_1 < 0, \\ w_1 & \text{if } w_1 \in [0, 1], \\ 1 & \text{if } w_1 > 1. \end{cases}$$

Hence, if the global minimum is outside $[0, 1]$, en embargo on short-selling means that an investor wishing to minimise his/her risk should put all his/her funds into one of the two assets.

## 2.5 Adding a risk-free security

All portfolios built of the risk-free asset (with rate of return $R$) and any other asset are represented by a straight half-line starting from $(0, R)$ and passing though the corresponding points on the $(\sigma, \mu)$-plane (see Figure 2.6). The new feasible region is thus obtained by taking any point on the attainable set and linking it with the risk-free asset, as shown in Figure 2.8. To find the new efficient frontier we seek a line with the highest slope according to the preference relation. Note that it is reasonable to make the following restriction: the risk-free return is smaller than the expected return of the risk-minimising portfolio. Under this assumption there is a unique portfolio on the efficient frontier, called the **market portfolio**, such that the line with the highest slope passes through it (see Figure 2.9). This optimal line, called the **capital market line**, is tangent to the efficient frontier (as follows from the elementary geometric properties of hyperbolas). Denoting

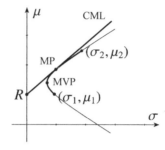

**Figure 2.9** The minimum variance portfolio (MVP), the market portfolio (MP), and the capital market line (CML).

the expected return of the market portfolio by $\mu_m$ and its risk by $\sigma_m$, the capital market line is given by

$$\mu = R + \frac{\mu_m - R}{\sigma_m}\sigma. \tag{2.15}$$

**Theorem 2.10**
*The weights of the market portfolio are* $\mathbf{m} = (w, 1 - w)$, *with*

$$w = \frac{c}{c + d}, \qquad 1 - w = \frac{d}{c + d}, \tag{2.16}$$

*where*

$$c = \sigma_2^2(\mu_1 - R) - \sigma_{12}(\mu_2 - R),$$
$$d = \sigma_1^2(\mu_2 - R) - \sigma_{12}(\mu_1 - R).$$

*Proof*   See page 33.                                                       □

**Corollary 2.11**
*The formulae (2.16) for the weights of the market portfolio can be written in matrix notation as*

$$\mathbf{m} = \frac{C^{-1}(\mu - R\mathbf{1})}{\mathbf{1}^{\mathsf{T}}C^{-1}(\mu - R\mathbf{1})}, \tag{2.17}$$

*where C is the covariance matrix,* $\mu = (\mu_1, \mu_2)$, *and* $\mathbf{1} = (1, 1)$.

---

**Exercise 2.10**   Verify that (2.16) and (2.17) are equivalent.

---

The following argument illustrates the possible practical relevance of the market portfolio.

Suppose that the market consists of two securities and suppose that the investors make their decisions on the basis of the expected returns and the covariance matrix, assuming in addition that they all use the same numerical values (returns, variances and covariance for the assets). If they all behave rationally, they perform the above computations and all arrive at the same market portfolio. They may choose different portfolios on the capital market line, but they all invest in the two given components in the same proportions. We conclude that, for each asset, its weight in the market portfolio represents its value as a proportion of the total value of the market.

To see this consider an example. Asset A is represented by 1000 shares at 20 dollars each, asset B by 500 shares at 40 dollars each, so each asset represents 50% of the market. If the investors have these assets in any other proportion, this leads to a contradiction with the fact that they all should have the same portfolio. Should any have above 50% of asset A, say, this would leave some other investors unsatisfied, since they wish to get more A than is available, and to sell some unwanted B. This would result in excess supply of B and excess demand of A, which would alter the prices, the expected returns and consequently the weights on the market portfolio. For this argument to be valid we have to assume that the market is in equilibrium.

**Example 2.12**
Assume that the covariance matrix $C$, the vector of expected returns $\mu$, and the risk-free return $R$ are given. Assume also that an investor wishes to spend $V$ and that the aim is to achieve an expected return equal to a given rate $m$. The question is how much he should spend on the risky assets, and how much he should invest risk-free.

First we compute $\mathbf{m}$ using (2.16). We can then compute the expected return of the market portfolio using (2.9)

$$\mu_\mathbf{m} = \mathbf{m}^\mathrm{T} \mu.$$

Optimal investments lie on the capital market line. The investor needs to hold a combination of the market portfolio and the risk-free security. We assume that he spends $\lambda V$ on the market portfolio and invests $(1 - \lambda) V$ risk-free. The desired $\lambda$ can be computed from the expected return of the position

$$\lambda \mu_\mathbf{m} + (1 - \lambda) R = m,$$

giving

$$\lambda = \frac{m - R}{\mu_\mathbf{m} - R}.$$

Since the investor spends $\lambda V$ on the market portfolio, the vector

$$\begin{pmatrix} v_1 \\ v_2 \end{pmatrix} = \lambda V \mathbf{m},$$

gives us the amount $v_1$ invested in the first asset, and $v_2$ invested in the second asset. As mentioned above, $(1 - \lambda) V$ is invested risk-free.

---

**Exercise 2.11**    Perform an analogous argument to the one in Example 2.12, for an investor who wishes to have the investment risk equal to a given $\sigma$ (instead of requiring that the expected return is $m$).

---

## 2.6  Indifference curves

The dominance relation, where we prefer portfolios lying to the left upper side of the $(\sigma, \mu)$-plane, does not help us choose between two assets where one has higher expected return and higher risk, and the other is less risky but with lower return. It seems impossible to extend the relation to solve this decision problem so that this extension would be accepted by all investors. The relation is based on risk aversion, but the investors who, as assumed, share this attitude, may differ in the intensity of their aversion. An investor who is sensitive to risk may require much higher returns as a compensation for increased exposure. Another investor may be cornered, forced to accept risk to earn the return needed to fulfil the requirements created by his circumstances, or may be just less sensitive to risk. It is inevitable that we have to allow for the modelling of individual preferences.

Let us fix our attention on one particular investor, and fix one particular asset (or portfolio of assets). We assume that this investor can answer the following question: which assets are equally as attractive as the fixed one? The answer provides us with a certain set of assets. Since the preference relation is valid, two assets with the same expected returns and different

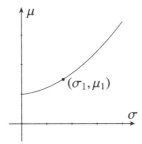

**Figure 2.10** An indifference curve for $(\sigma_1, \mu_1)$.

risk will never be equally attractive; nor will be two assets with the same risk but different expected returns. Thus the intersection of this set by any line parallel to any of the axes can contain at most one element. So it is a graph of an increasing function. We assume in addition that this function is convex for each investor – in other words, to retain his peace of mind, the investor demands that a unit increase of risk be offset by more than one unit increase in return, as shown in Figure 2.10 – and we call it an **indifference curve.**

We assume that indifference curves are level sets of a function

$$u : \mathbb{R}^2 \to \mathbb{R}.$$

We assume that a curve $\{u = c_2\}$ lies above $\{u = c_1\}$ for $c_1 < c_2$. In other words, the higher the value of $u$, the higher the investor's satisfaction with the investment. Given a set of attainable portfolios, an investor chooses the one placed on the best indifference curve. It is geometrically obvious as a result of convexity of the curves that the optimal portfolio is at the tangency point with the capital market line, for some indifference curve, as shown in Figure 2.11(a).

For another investor, who is less risk averse, that is, who has less steep indifference curves, the optimal portfolio may be different, as in Figure 2.11(b). It lies further to the right, which agrees with our intuition regarding the risk preferences of this investor.

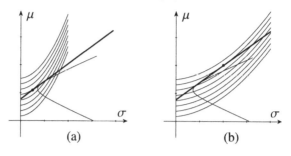

**Figure 2.11** Indifference curves and optimal investment for an investor with high risk aversion (a), and lower risk aversion (b).

### Example 2.13

Assume that the covariance matrix $C$, the vector of expected returns $\mu$, and the risk-free return $R$ are given, and that an investor's indifference curves are the level sets of the function

$$u(\sigma,\mu) = \mu - \frac{a}{2}\sigma^2. \qquad (2.18)$$

We show how the investor should spend $V$ to maximise $u$. The indifference curves are the level sets $u(\sigma,\mu) = c$, so that we obtain $\mu = c + \frac{a}{2}\sigma^2$, which is convex and has slope $a\sigma$.

Using (2.17), (2.9) and (2.10) we can find the market portfolio $\mathbf{m}$, its expected return $\mu_{\mathbf{m}}$ and variance $\sigma_{\mathbf{m}}^2$. Since the slope $a\sigma$ of the indifference curve needs to match the slope of the capital market line, the tangency point can be found by solving the system of two linear equations

$$\mu = R + \frac{\mu_{\mathbf{m}} - R}{\sigma_{\mathbf{m}}}\sigma,$$

$$a\sigma = \frac{\mu_{\mathbf{m}} - R}{\sigma_{\mathbf{m}}}.$$

This means that

$$\mu = R + \frac{1}{a}\left(\frac{\mu_{\mathbf{m}} - R}{\sigma_{\mathbf{m}}}\right)^2.$$

We can now determine how to divide $V$ amongst the assets using the same method as in Example 2.12.

**Exercise 2.12** Consider two risky securities and a risk-free asset with the following parameters:

$$\mu_1 = 10\%, \qquad \sigma_1 = 0.1, \qquad \rho_{12} = -0.5,$$
$$\mu_2 = 20\%, \qquad \sigma_2 = 0.3, \qquad R = 5\%.$$

Assume that the investors's indifference curves are given by (2.18) with $a = 5$. How should the investor divide $V = 3000$ amongst the assets?

We shall return to indifference curves in Chapter 6, where we will discuss their relation to utility functions.

## 2.7 Proofs

### Theorem 2.7
*If $\mu_1 \neq \mu_2$ and $\rho_{12} \in (-1, 1)$, then the attainable set is a hyperbola with its centre on the vertical axis.*

*Proof* For a more familiar notation we introduce the letters $x, y$ for the coordinates so that we have the following description of the attainable set:

$$y = w\mu_1 + (1 - w)\mu_2, \tag{2.19}$$
$$x^2 = w^2\sigma_1^2 + (1 - w)^2\sigma_2^2 + 2w(1 - w)\sigma_{12}. \tag{2.20}$$

The goal of further computations is to convert the above system of equations to the form

$$\frac{(x - h)^2}{a^2} - \frac{(y - k)^2}{b^2} = 1, \tag{2.21}$$

from which we will be able to read off the properties of the hyperbola (see Figure 2.12).

Solving (2.19) for $w$

$$w = \frac{y - \mu_2}{\mu_1 - \mu_2}$$

(note the relevance of the assumption $\mu_1 \neq \mu_2$) and inserting into (2.20), we get

$$x^2 = \frac{1}{A}[(y - \mu_2)^2\sigma_1^2 + (\mu_1 - y)^2\sigma_2^2 + 2(y - \mu_2)(\mu_1 - y)\sigma_{12}],$$

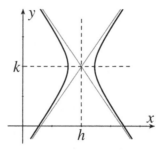

**Figure 2.12** The hyperbola $\frac{(x-h)^2}{a^2} - \frac{(y-k)^2}{b^2} = 1$.

where $A = (\mu_1 - \mu_2)^2 > 0$. Simple computation gives

$$x^2 = \frac{1}{A}[By^2 - 2Cy + D], \tag{2.22}$$

where

$$B = \sigma_1^2 + \sigma_2^2 - 2\sigma_{12},$$
$$C = \sigma_1^2\mu_2 + \sigma_2^2\mu_1 - \sigma_{12}(\mu_1 + \mu_2),$$
$$D = \sigma_1^2\mu_2^2 + \sigma_2^2\mu_1^2 - 2\sigma_{12}\mu_1\mu_2.$$

Observe, that $B > 0$ if $\rho_{12} < 1$, since $\sigma_1^2 + \sigma_2^2 - 2\sigma_{12} > \sigma_1^2 + \sigma_2^2 - 2\sigma_1\sigma_2 \geq 0$.
We can write

$$By^2 - 2Cy + D = B\left[y^2 - 2y\frac{C}{B} + \frac{D}{B}\right]$$
$$= B\left[(y - \frac{C}{B})^2 - \frac{C^2}{B^2} + \frac{D}{B}\right]$$
$$= B(y - k)^2 + c,$$

with $k = \frac{C}{B}$ and $c = \frac{1}{B}\left(BD - C^2\right)$. Substituting into (2.22) gives

$$x^2 = \frac{1}{A}\left[B(y - k)^2 + c\right],$$

hence

$$\frac{x^2}{\frac{c}{A}} - \frac{(y - k)^2}{\frac{c}{B}} = 1. \tag{2.23}$$

We can see that we have obtained the desired hyperbola equation (2.21), with $h = 0$, meaning that the center of the hyperbola lies on the vertical axis (see Figure 2.12).

One loose end to tie up is to show that $c \neq 0$, as otherwise we would be dividing by zero in (2.23). A simple but tedious computation shows that

$$BD - C^2 = A\sigma_1^2\sigma_2^2(1 - \rho_{12}^2).$$

Since $\rho_{12} \in (-1, 1)$, $B > 0$ and $A > 0$,

$$c = \frac{1}{B}\left(BD - C^2\right) = \frac{A}{B}\sigma_1^2\sigma_2^2(1 - \rho_{12}^2) > 0.$$

$\square$

---

**Exercise 2.13** Show that the asymptotes of the hyperbola

$$\frac{(x - h)^2}{a^2} - \frac{(y - k)^2}{b^2} = 1$$

are

$$\frac{x - h}{a} \pm \frac{y - k}{b} = 0.$$

---

**Theorem 2.10**
*The weights of the market portfolio are* $\mathbf{m} = (w, 1 - w)$, *with*

$$w = \frac{c}{c + d}, \quad 1 - w = \frac{d}{c + d},$$

*where*

$$c = \sigma_2^2(\mu_1 - R) - \sigma_{12}(\mu_2 - R),$$
$$d = \sigma_1^2(\mu_2 - R) - \sigma_{12}(\mu_1 - R).$$

*Proof* For a portfolio $(w, 1 - w)$, we denote its expected return by $\mu(w)$, and standard deviation by $\sigma(w)$. Optimisation is based on maximising the slope coefficient:

$$s(w) = \frac{\mu(w) - R}{\sigma(w)}.$$

To this end it is necessary and sufficient to solve

$$s'(w) = 0.$$

We have

$$s'(w) = \frac{\mu'(w)\sigma(w) - (\mu(w) - R)\sigma'(w)}{\sigma^2(w)}.$$

Since

$$\sigma'(w) = \left( \sqrt{\sigma^2(w)} \right)' = \frac{1}{2\sqrt{\sigma^2(w)}} (\sigma^2(w))' = \frac{1}{2\sigma(w)} (\sigma^2(w))',$$

the equation $s'(w) = 0$ reduces to

$$2\mu'(w)\sigma^2(w) - (\mu(w) - R)(\sigma^2(w))' = 0,$$

that is

$$(\mu_1 - \mu_2)(w^2\sigma_1^2 + (1-w)^2\sigma_2^2 + 2w(1-w)\sigma_{12})$$
$$-(w\mu_1 + (1-w)\mu_2 - R)(w\sigma_1^2 - (1-w)\sigma_2^2 + (1-2w)\sigma_{12}) = 0.$$

This is in fact a linear equation in $w$ since all terms involving $w^2$ cancel out. Elementary, but tedious computations give

$$w = \frac{c}{c+d}, \quad 1 - w = \frac{d}{c+d},$$

which concludes the proof. $\qquad\qquad\qquad\qquad\qquad\qquad\qquad\qquad$ □

# 3

---

# Lagrange multipliers

---

The mean-variance analysis of asset portfolios carried out in the previous chapter was greatly simplified by considering portfolios of only two assets. This meant that the portfolio weights involved only a single variable, making basic calculus techniques available for finding the portfolio of minimum variance. For portfolios of more than two assets this no longer applies. We will need a method that will allows us to find minima of functions of many variables under constraints. (In portfolio theory the first natural constraint is that all weights need to add up to one.)

In this chapter we digress a little from portfolio theory. We present a general method that locates potential extreme points of functions under constraints, and, in a special case that suffices for our intended applications, enables us to classify them as maxima or minima. It turns out that the minimisation problem provides a system of equations whose solution provides a candidate for the minimum. The 'method of Lagrange multipliers' is a standard tool in advanced calculus, but the proofs we provide are frequently only sketched in standard textbooks.

## 3.1  Motivating examples

The aim of this section is to provide the underlying geometric intuition for the method.

We consider two functions

$$f : \mathbb{R}^2 \to \mathbb{R},$$
$$g : \mathbb{R}^2 \to \mathbb{R},$$

and show how to find solutions of the following problem:
Find

$$\min f(x, y),$$
$$\text{under the constraint: } g(x, y) = 0. \tag{3.1}$$

We start with a simple example.

**Example 3.1**
Consider

$$f(x, y) = x^2 + y^2,$$
$$g(x, y) = \frac{1}{2}x + \frac{1}{2}y - \frac{1}{2}.$$

Basic arguments (say, by substituting $y = 1 - x$ into $f(x, y)$ and computing a derivative with respect to $x$) lead to the solution

$$x^* = y^* = \frac{1}{2}. \tag{3.2}$$

We now present an alternative approach. We first observe that one of the level curves $\{(x, y) : f(x, y) = r^2\}$ (which are circles of radius $r$, as shown in Figure 3.1) is tangent at the point $(x^*, y^*)$ to the line $\{(x, y) : g(x, y) = 0\}$. Since the gradients

$$\nabla f(x, y) = \begin{bmatrix} \frac{\partial f}{\partial x}(x, y) \\ \frac{\partial f}{\partial y}(x, y) \end{bmatrix} = \begin{bmatrix} 2x \\ 2y \end{bmatrix},$$

$$\nabla g(x, y) = \begin{bmatrix} \frac{\partial g}{\partial x}(x, y) \\ \frac{\partial g}{\partial y}(x, y) \end{bmatrix} = \begin{bmatrix} \frac{1}{2} \\ \frac{1}{2} \end{bmatrix},$$

are orthogonal to the level curves, the vectors $\nabla f(x^*, y^*)$ and $\nabla g(x^*, y^*)$ should be collinear. This means that there should exist a number $\lambda \in \mathbb{R}$ such that we have the following system of two equations:

$$\nabla f(x, y) - \lambda \nabla g(x, y) = 0. \tag{3.3}$$

The idea is to solve (3.3) instead of (3.1); in other words, we solve a system of equations, instead of solving a minimisation problem.

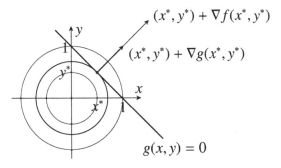

**Figure 3.1** The level curves $\{f = r^2\}$ for $r = 1$ (outer circle), $r = \frac{1}{\sqrt{2}}$ (middle circle) and $r = \frac{1}{2}$ (inner circle), together with the gradients $\nabla f$ and $\nabla g$, attached at $(x^*, y^*)$.

Together with the constraint $g(x, y) = 0$, (3.3) leads to the linear system

$$2x - \frac{1}{2}\lambda = 0,$$

$$2y - \frac{1}{2}\lambda = 0, \qquad\qquad (3.4)$$

$$\frac{1}{2}x + \frac{1}{2}y - \frac{1}{2} = 0,$$

with the unique solution

$$x^* = y^* = \frac{1}{2}, \qquad \lambda^* = 2.$$

The points $x^*$ and $y^*$ found by this method are the same as those found in (3.2).

In Figure 3.2 we see that in this example the point $(x^*, y^*)$ is the only point on $\{g(x, y) = 0\}$, at which $\nabla f$ and $\nabla g$ are collinear, hence the only point where (3.3) can hold.

**Exercise 3.1** Solve (3.4) using Cramer's rule.

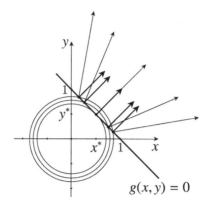

**Figure 3.2** Gradients $\nabla f$ (longer arrows) and $\nabla g$ (shorter arrows), attached at $(x^*, y^*)$ and at four other points on $g(x, y) = 0$.

Example 3.1 suggests that instead of solving the problem (3.1) we can look for a solution of the system of equations

$$\nabla f(x, y) - \lambda \nabla g(x, y) = 0, \qquad (3.5)$$

$$g(x, y) = 0.$$

Solving a system of equations can turn out to be easier than minimising a function under constraints.

We now test how this works on an example from portfolio theory that was discussed in Chapter 2.

**Example 3.2**
We consider the problem of finding the minimum variance portfolio when given two risky assets, as in Chapter 2. To use the same notation as in (3.5), we write $x$ and $y$ instead of $w_1$ and $w_2$, respectively, and take

$$f(x, y) = x^2 \sigma_1^2 + y^2 \sigma_2^2 + 2xy\sigma_{12},$$

$$g(x, y) = x + y - 1.$$

The constraint $g(x, y) = 0$ ensures that $x$ and $y$ add up to one, making the pair $(x, y)$ a well defined portfolio. The function $f$ gives its variance.

The gradients are

$$\nabla f(x,y) = \begin{bmatrix} 2\sigma_1^2 x + 2\sigma_{12} y \\ 2\sigma_{12} x + 2\sigma_2^2 y \end{bmatrix},$$

$$\nabla g(x,y) = \begin{bmatrix} 1 \\ 1 \end{bmatrix}.$$

Equation (3.5) leads to

$$\begin{aligned}
2\sigma_1^2 x + 2\sigma_{12} y - \lambda &= 0, \\
2\sigma_{12} x + 2\sigma_2^2 y - \lambda &= 0, \\
x + y - 1 &= 0.
\end{aligned} \tag{3.6}$$

This system can be solved, (using Cramer's rule, for example) to obtain

$$\begin{aligned}
x^* &= \frac{\sigma_2^2 - \sigma_{12}}{\sigma_1^2 + \sigma_2^2 - 2\sigma_{12}}, \\
y^* &= \frac{\sigma_1^2 - \sigma_{12}}{\sigma_1^2 + \sigma_2^2 - 2\sigma_{12}}, \\
\lambda^* &= 2\frac{\sigma_1^2 \sigma_2^2 - \sigma_{12}^2}{\sigma_1^2 + \sigma_2^2 - 2\sigma_{12}}.
\end{aligned} \tag{3.7}$$

We see that $x^*$ and $y^*$ are identical to the weights $w_1$ and $w_2$ obtained in Theorem 2.8.

Figure 3.3 contains a numerically obtained plot of the point $(x^*, y^*)$, the level curve $\{f(x,y) = \sigma_{w_{min}}^2\}$ and the line $\{g(x,y) = 0\}$. We see that, as expected, we have a point of tangency at $(x^*, y^*)$, which is the minimum variance portfolio.

---

**Exercise 3.2**   Verify that (3.7) is a solution of (3.6).

---

**Exercise 3.3**   Recreate the plot from Figure 3.3.

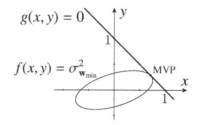

**Figure 3.3** The tangency of $\{f(x,y) = \sigma^2_{\mathbf{w}_{min}}\}$ and $\{x+y = 1\}$ at the minimum variance portfolio (computed for $\sigma_1 = 0.1$, $\sigma_2 = 0.2$ and $\rho_{12} = -0.5$).

## 3.2 Constrained extrema

The examples from the previous section have been considered on the plane. It turns out that a similar approach can be used in higher dimensions, and that we can consider more complicated constraints.

Our objective in this section is to show how to solve the following general **constrained minimisation** problem:
Find

$$\min f(\mathbf{v}),$$
$$\text{under the constraints: } \mathbf{g}(\mathbf{v}) = \mathbf{0}, \tag{3.8}$$

where

$$f : \mathbb{R}^n \to \mathbb{R},$$
$$\mathbf{g} : \mathbb{R}^n \to \mathbb{R}^k.$$

We will provide necessary and, in the special case of quadratic forms, sufficient conditions for a solution to this problem.

To keep better track of dimensions, we use a bold font whenever we are dealing with vectors, and the normal font when dealing with numbers. Note that in stating the problem above we used $f$ for a function taking values in $\mathbb{R}$ and $\mathbf{g}$ for a function

$$\mathbf{g}(\mathbf{v}) = (g_1(\mathbf{v}), \ldots, g_k(\mathbf{v}))$$

taking values in $\mathbb{R}^k$.

For the reader's convenience we review some notations from multi-variable calculus. We use the notation $\mathbf{g}'(\mathbf{v})$ to denote the $k \times n$ **Jacobian matrix**

$$\mathbf{g}'(\mathbf{v}) = \begin{bmatrix} \frac{\partial g_1}{\partial x_1}(\mathbf{v}) & \frac{\partial g_1}{\partial x_2}(\mathbf{v}) & \cdots & \frac{\partial g_1}{\partial x_n}(\mathbf{v}) \\ \frac{\partial g_2}{\partial x_1}(\mathbf{v}) & \frac{\partial g_2}{\partial x_2}(\mathbf{v}) & \cdots & \frac{\partial g_2}{\partial x_n}(\mathbf{v}) \\ \vdots & \vdots & & \vdots \\ \frac{\partial g_k}{\partial x_1}(\mathbf{v}) & \frac{\partial g_k}{\partial x_2}(\mathbf{v}) & \cdots & \frac{\partial g_k}{\partial x_n}(\mathbf{v}) \end{bmatrix}.$$

We say that $\mathbf{g} : \mathbb{R}^n \to \mathbb{R}^k$ is **continuously differentiable** if all the entries in its Jacobian matrix are continuous functions.

For a function $f : \mathbb{R}^n \to \mathbb{R}$, the Jacobian matrix is

$$f'(\mathbf{v}) = \begin{bmatrix} \frac{\partial f}{\partial x_1}(\mathbf{v}) & \frac{\partial f}{\partial x_2}(\mathbf{v}) & \cdots & \frac{\partial f}{\partial x_n}(\mathbf{v}) \end{bmatrix}.$$

At times it will be more convenient to use a vector instead of a $1 \times n$ matrix. We therefore introduce the notation $\nabla f(\mathbf{v})$ for the **gradient**

$$\nabla f(\mathbf{v}) = \begin{bmatrix} \frac{\partial f}{\partial x_1}(\mathbf{v}) \\ \vdots \\ \frac{\partial f}{\partial x_n}(\mathbf{v}) \end{bmatrix}.$$

The necessary condition for a continuously differentiable $f : \mathbb{R}^n \to \mathbb{R}$ to have a minimum at $\mathbf{v}^*$, under the constraint that $\mathbf{g}(\mathbf{v}^*) = \mathbf{0}$, for some continuously differentiable function $\mathbf{g} : \mathbb{R}^n \to \mathbb{R}^k$, can now be stated as follows.

**Theorem 3.3**
*If $\mathbf{v}^*$ is a solution of the problem (3.8), and $\mathbf{g}'(\mathbf{v}^*)$ is a matrix of rank $k$, then there exists a sequence of numbers $\lambda_1, \ldots, \lambda_k \in \mathbb{R}$ such that*

$$\nabla f(\mathbf{v}^*) - (\lambda_1 \nabla g_1(\mathbf{v}^*) + \cdots + \lambda_k \nabla g_k(\mathbf{v}^*)) = \mathbf{0}. \tag{3.9}$$

*Proof*  Following a brief review of standard auxiliary results, the proof is given on page 45. □

The $\lambda_1, \ldots, \lambda_k$ from Theorem 3.3 are referred to as **Lagrange multipliers,** and the function

$$L(\mathbf{v}) = \nabla f(\mathbf{v}^*) - (\lambda_1 \nabla g_1(\mathbf{v}^*) + \cdots + \lambda_k \nabla g_k(\mathbf{v}^*))$$

is the **Lagrangian** of the constrained optimisation problem (3.8).

We emphasise that Theorem 3.3 only provides necessary conditions for a minimum of $f$. Even if (3.9) holds for some $\mathbf{v}^*$, it does not necessarily imply that $\mathbf{v}^*$ is a minimum. This is similar in spirit to searching for a local minimum of a function $f : \mathbb{R} \to \mathbb{R}$, where we first find points $x^*$ satisfying

$f'(x^*) = 0$, but to confirm $f$ has a minimum at such a point, additional conditions need to be checked. Similarly, Theorem 3.3 is a handy tool for finding candidates for a solution of problem (3.8). To prove that such a candidate is indeed a solution one usually needs additional information.

---

**Exercise 3.4**   Show that for

$$f(x, y, z) = z,$$
$$g(x, y, z) = x^2 - y^2 + z^2 - 1,$$

the method of Lagrange multipliers does not establish a solution of (3.8).

---

**Exercise 3.5**   Show that for

$$f(x, y, z) = x + y + z,$$
$$g(x, y, z) = x^2 + y^2 + z^2 - 1,$$

the system of equations (3.9) has two solutions, of which only one is the solution of (3.8).

---

An analogous result to Theorem 3.3 can be formulated for a problem in which we seek a maximum instead of a minimum. The method also works for local minima and maxima. The resulting necessary condition in these cases remains the same as (3.9).

---

**Exercise 3.6**   Find the maximal volume of a rectangular box, whose edges are parallel to the axes, that fits entirely inside the ellipsoid

$$\frac{x^2}{a^2} + \frac{y^2}{b^2} + \frac{z^2}{c^2} = 1.$$

---

In special cases the necessary condition (3.9) turns out to be sufficient for $\mathbf{v}^*$ to be a solution of the problem. Before stating this result we need to review some further concepts.

For a function $f : \mathbb{R}^n \to \mathbb{R}$, we call the $n \times n$ matrix

$$H(f, \mathbf{v}) = \begin{bmatrix} \frac{\partial^2 f}{\partial x_1 \partial x_1}(\mathbf{v}) & \frac{\partial^2 f}{\partial x_1 \partial x_2}(\mathbf{v}) & \cdots & \frac{\partial^2 f}{\partial x_1 \partial x_n}(\mathbf{v}) \\ \frac{\partial^2 f}{\partial x_2 \partial x_1}(\mathbf{v}) & \frac{\partial^2 f}{\partial x_2 \partial x_2}(\mathbf{v}) & \cdots & \frac{\partial^2 f}{\partial x_2 \partial x_n}(\mathbf{v}) \\ \vdots & \vdots & & \vdots \\ \frac{\partial^2 f}{\partial x_n \partial x_1}(\mathbf{v}) & \frac{\partial^2 f}{\partial x_n \partial x_2}(\mathbf{v}) & \cdots & \frac{\partial^2 f}{\partial x_n \partial x_n}(\mathbf{v}) \end{bmatrix}$$

the **Hessian matrix** of $f$ at $\mathbf{v}$. A function is said to be **twice continuously differentiable** if all the entries in its Hessian matrix are continuous functions with respect to $\mathbf{v}$.

**Theorem 3.4**
*Assume that $f : \mathbb{R}^n \to \mathbb{R}$ is twice continuously differentiable, and that for any $\mathbf{v} \in \mathbb{R}^n$ the Hessian $H(f, \mathbf{v})$ is a positive semidefinite matrix, meaning that*

$$\mathbf{w}^\mathrm{T} H(f, \mathbf{v}) \mathbf{w} \geq 0, \tag{3.10}$$

*for any $\mathbf{w} \in \mathbb{R}^n$. Assume also that*

$$\mathbf{g}(\mathbf{v}) = A\mathbf{v} - \mathbf{c},$$

*where $A$ is a $k \times n$ matrix and $\mathbf{c} \in \mathbb{R}^k$.*

*If we can find a sequence of numbers $\lambda_1, \ldots, \lambda_k \in \mathbb{R}$ and a point $\mathbf{v}^* \in \mathbb{R}^n$ such that (3.9) is satisfied, then $\mathbf{v}^*$ is a solution of the problem (3.8).*

*Proof* See page 46. □

---

**Exercise 3.7** Show that if the inequality in (3.10) is reversed, then condition (3.9) implies that $\mathbf{v}^*$ is a solution of the following constrained maximisation problem:

$$\max f(\mathbf{v}),$$
under the constraints: $\mathbf{g}(\mathbf{v}) = \mathbf{0}.$

## 3.3 Proofs

Our proof of Theorem 3.3 depends on the implicit function theorem, which is a classical result in analysis. We state this theorem without proof,[1] after introducing some notation.

For

$$\mathbf{g} = (g_1, \ldots, g_k) : \mathbb{R}^l \times \mathbb{R}^m \to \mathbb{R}^k$$

and $(\mathbf{x}, \mathbf{y}) \in \mathbb{R}^l \times \mathbb{R}^m$, $\mathbf{x} = (x_1, \ldots x_l)$ and $\mathbf{y} = (y_1, \ldots y_m)$ we write $\frac{\partial \mathbf{g}}{\partial \mathbf{x}}$ and $\frac{\partial \mathbf{g}}{\partial \mathbf{y}}$ for the $k \times l$ (resp. $k \times m$) matrices

$$\frac{\partial \mathbf{g}}{\partial \mathbf{x}}(\mathbf{x}, \mathbf{y}) = \begin{bmatrix} \frac{\partial g_1}{\partial x_1}(\mathbf{x}, \mathbf{y}) & \frac{\partial g_1}{\partial x_2}(\mathbf{x}, \mathbf{y}) & \cdots & \frac{\partial g_1}{\partial x_l}(\mathbf{x}, \mathbf{y}) \\ \vdots & \vdots & & \vdots \\ \frac{\partial g_k}{\partial x_1}(\mathbf{x}, \mathbf{y}) & \frac{\partial g_k}{\partial x_2}(\mathbf{x}, \mathbf{y}) & \cdots & \frac{\partial g_k}{\partial x_l}(\mathbf{x}, \mathbf{y}) \end{bmatrix},$$

$$\frac{\partial \mathbf{g}}{\partial \mathbf{y}}(\mathbf{x}, \mathbf{y}) = \begin{bmatrix} \frac{\partial g_1}{\partial y_1}(\mathbf{x}, \mathbf{y}) & \frac{\partial g_1}{\partial y_2}(\mathbf{x}, \mathbf{y}) & \cdots & \frac{\partial g_1}{\partial y_m}(\mathbf{x}, \mathbf{y}) \\ \vdots & \vdots & & \vdots \\ \frac{\partial g_k}{\partial y_1}(\mathbf{x}, \mathbf{y}) & \frac{\partial g_k}{\partial y_2}(\mathbf{x}, \mathbf{y}) & \cdots & \frac{\partial g_k}{\partial y_m}(\mathbf{x}, \mathbf{y}) \end{bmatrix}.$$

**Theorem 3.5 (Implicit function theorem)**
*Consider $n > k$ and a continuously differentiable function*

$$\mathbf{g} = (g_1, \ldots, g_k) : \mathbb{R}^{n-k} \times \mathbb{R}^k \to \mathbb{R}^k.$$

*Assume that at a point $(\mathbf{x}^*, \mathbf{y}^*) \in \mathbb{R}^{n-k} \times \mathbb{R}^k$ we have*

$$\mathbf{g}(\mathbf{x}^*, \mathbf{y}^*) = \mathbf{0},$$

*and that the matrix $\frac{\partial \mathbf{g}}{\partial \mathbf{y}}(\mathbf{x}^*, \mathbf{y}^*)$ is invertible. Then there exists a neighbourhood $U \times V \subset \mathbb{R}^{n-k} \times \mathbb{R}^k$ of $(\mathbf{x}^*, \mathbf{y}^*)$ and a continuously differentiable function*

$$\mathbf{h} : U \to V,$$

*such that*

$$\mathbf{g}(\mathbf{x}, \mathbf{h}(\mathbf{x})) = \mathbf{0} \qquad \text{for all } \mathbf{x} \in U.$$

*Moreover, for any $\mathbf{v} \in U \times V$, if $\mathbf{g}(\mathbf{v}) = \mathbf{0}$ then $\mathbf{v} = (\mathbf{x}, \mathbf{h}(\mathbf{x}))$ for some $\mathbf{x} \in U$.*

**Corollary 3.6**
*For the function $\mathbf{h}$ from Theorem 3.5*

$$\mathbf{h}'(\mathbf{x}) = -\left(\frac{\partial \mathbf{g}}{\partial \mathbf{y}}(\mathbf{x}, \mathbf{h}(\mathbf{x}))\right)^{-1} \frac{\partial \mathbf{g}}{\partial \mathbf{x}}(\mathbf{x}, \mathbf{h}(\mathbf{x})).$$

[1] For proofs of the standard multi-variable calculus results used below, see (e.g.) T. M. Apostol, *Mathematical Analysis*, 2nd edition, Addison-Wesley 1974.

*Proof*  Since $g(x, h(x)) = 0$, by computing the derivative with respect to $x$ we obtain from the chain rule that

$$\frac{\partial g}{\partial x}(x, h(x)) + \frac{\partial g}{\partial y}(x, h(x))h'(x) = 0.$$

In this identity, $\frac{\partial g}{\partial x}(x, h(x))$, $h'(x)$ and $0$ denote $k \times (n - k)$ matrices. Since $\frac{\partial g}{\partial y}(x, h(x))$ is a $k \times k$ matrix, it can be inverted. The claim now follows by rearranging so that $h'(x)$ is on the left-hand side.  □

We are now ready to prove Theorem 3.3.

**Theorem 3.3**
*If $v^*$ is a solution of the problem (3.8), and $g'(v^*)$ is a matrix of rank $k$, then there exists a sequence of numbers $\lambda_1, \ldots, \lambda_k \in \mathbb{R}$ such that*

$$\nabla f(v^*) - (\lambda_1 \nabla g_1(v^*) + \cdots + \lambda_k \nabla g_k(v^*)) = 0. \tag{3.9}$$

*Proof*  Since $g'(v^*)$ is of rank $k$, there exists a $k$-dimensional vector $y$ such that $\frac{\partial g}{\partial y}(v^*)$ is invertible. We can always renumber the coordinates so that $v = (x, y)$ with $x \in \mathbb{R}^{n-k}$ and $y \in \mathbb{R}^k$.

By the implicit function theorem, we know that there exists a function $h$ such that

$$g(x, h(x)) = 0.$$

Since $v^* = (x^*, y^*)$ is a solution of problem (3.8), $x^*$ is a minimum of $f(x, h(x))$, meaning that the derivative of $f(x, h(x))$ with respect to $x$ is zero at $x^*$. Applying Corollary 3.6, this gives

$$\begin{aligned}
0 &= \frac{\partial f}{\partial x}(v^*) + \frac{\partial f}{\partial y}(v^*)h'(x^*) \\
&= \frac{\partial f}{\partial x}(v^*) - \frac{\partial f}{\partial y}(v^*)\left(\frac{\partial g}{\partial y}(v^*)\right)^{-1}\frac{\partial g}{\partial x}(v^*).
\end{aligned} \tag{3.11}$$

We define a $1 \times k$ matrix $\Lambda$ by

$$\Lambda = \begin{bmatrix} \lambda_1 & \lambda_2 & \cdots & \lambda_k \end{bmatrix} = \frac{\partial f}{\partial y}(v^*)\left(\frac{\partial g}{\partial y}(v^*)\right)^{-1}.$$

From (3.11) it follows that

$$\frac{\partial f}{\partial x}(v^*) = \Lambda \frac{\partial g}{\partial x}(v^*). \tag{3.12}$$

From the definition of $\Lambda$,

$$\frac{\partial f}{\partial y}(v^*) = \Lambda \frac{\partial g}{\partial y}(v^*). \tag{3.13}$$

Conditions (3.12) and (3.13) combined give (3.9). $\qquad$ □

The proof of Theorem 3.4 is based on a particular case of Taylor's theorem, which we state (without proof) in the following form:

### Theorem 3.7 (Taylor formula)

*Suppose that $f : \mathbb{R}^n \to \mathbb{R}$ is a twice continuously differentiable function. Then for any $\mathbf{v}, \mathbf{w} \in \mathbb{R}^n$ there exists a point $\boldsymbol{\xi}$ contained in the line segment joining $\mathbf{v}$ and $\mathbf{v} + \mathbf{w}$,*

$$\boldsymbol{\xi} \in \{\mathbf{v} + \alpha\mathbf{w} : \alpha \in [0, 1]\},$$

*such that*

$$f(\mathbf{v} + \mathbf{w}) = f(\mathbf{v}) + \nabla f(\mathbf{v}) \cdot \mathbf{w} + \frac{1}{2}\mathbf{w}^{\mathrm{T}}H(f, \boldsymbol{\xi})\mathbf{w},$$

*where the dot stands for the scalar product.*

We are now ready to prove Theorem 3.4.

### Theorem 3.4

*Assume that $f : \mathbb{R}^n \to \mathbb{R}$ is twice differentiable, and that for any $\mathbf{v} \in \mathbb{R}^n$ the Hessian $H(f, \mathbf{v})$ is a positive semidefinite matrix, meaning that*

$$\mathbf{w}^{\mathrm{T}}H(f, \mathbf{v})\mathbf{w} \geq 0, \tag{3.10}$$

*for any $\mathbf{w} \in \mathbb{R}^n$. Assume also that*

$$\mathbf{g}(\mathbf{v}) = A\mathbf{v} - \mathbf{c},$$

*where $A$ is a $k \times n$ matrix and $\mathbf{c} \in \mathbb{R}^k$.*

*If we can find a sequence of numbers $\lambda_1, \ldots, \lambda_k \in \mathbb{R}$ and a point $\mathbf{v}^* \in \mathbb{R}^n$ such that (3.9) is satisfied, then $\mathbf{v}^*$ is a solution of the problem (3.8).*

*Proof* Let us take any $\mathbf{v}$ satisfying $\mathbf{g}(\mathbf{v}) = \mathbf{0}$. We need to show that

$$f(\mathbf{v}) \geq f(\mathbf{v}^*).$$

Since $\mathbf{g}(\mathbf{v}) = A\mathbf{v} - \mathbf{c}$, using the notation $\lambda = (\lambda_1, \ldots, \lambda_k)$ we can write

$$\lambda_1 \nabla g_1(\mathbf{v}^*) + \cdots + \lambda_k \nabla g_k(\mathbf{v}^*) = A^{\mathrm{T}}\lambda. \tag{3.14}$$

Let $\mathbf{w} = \mathbf{v} - \mathbf{v}^*$. Since $\mathbf{g}(\mathbf{v}) = \mathbf{0}$ and $\mathbf{g}(\mathbf{v}^*) = \mathbf{0}$, we use the linearity of $A$ to obtain

$$\mathbf{0} = \mathbf{g}(\mathbf{v}) = \mathbf{g}(\mathbf{v}^* + \mathbf{w}) = A\mathbf{v}^* + A\mathbf{w} - \mathbf{c} = \mathbf{g}(\mathbf{v}^*) + A\mathbf{w} = A\mathbf{w}. \tag{3.15}$$

By the Taylor formula recalled in Theorem 3.7,

$$f(\mathbf{v}^* + \mathbf{w}) = f(\mathbf{v}^*) + \nabla f(\mathbf{v}^*) \cdot \mathbf{w} + \frac{1}{2}\mathbf{w}^{\mathrm{T}}H(f, \boldsymbol{\xi})\mathbf{w}, \tag{3.16}$$

for some point $\boldsymbol{\xi}$ on the line segment in $\mathbb{R}^n$ between $\mathbf{v}^*$ and $\mathbf{v}^* + \mathbf{w}$.

We can now compute

$$
\begin{aligned}
f(\mathbf{v}) &= f(\mathbf{v}^* + \mathbf{w}) \\
&= f(\mathbf{v}^*) + \nabla f(\mathbf{v}^*) \cdot \mathbf{w} + \tfrac{1}{2}\mathbf{w}^\mathrm{T} H(f, \boldsymbol{\xi})\mathbf{w} && \text{(from (3.16))} \\
&= f(\mathbf{v}^*) + A^\mathrm{T}\boldsymbol{\lambda} \cdot \mathbf{w} + \tfrac{1}{2}\mathbf{w}^\mathrm{T} H(f, \boldsymbol{\xi})\mathbf{w} && \text{(from (3.9) and (3.14))} \\
&= f(\mathbf{v}^*) + \left(A^\mathrm{T}\boldsymbol{\lambda}\right)^\mathrm{T} \mathbf{w} + \tfrac{1}{2}\mathbf{w}^\mathrm{T} H(f, \boldsymbol{\xi})\mathbf{w} \\
&= f(\mathbf{v}^*) + \boldsymbol{\lambda}^\mathrm{T} A\mathbf{w} + \tfrac{1}{2}\mathbf{w}^\mathrm{T} H(f, \boldsymbol{\xi})\mathbf{w} \\
&= f(\mathbf{v}^*) + \tfrac{1}{2}\mathbf{w}^\mathrm{T} H(f, \boldsymbol{\xi})\mathbf{w} && \text{(from (3.15))} \\
&\geq f(\mathbf{v}^*). && \text{(from (3.10))}
\end{aligned}
$$

We have proved that $\mathbf{v}^*$ is a (non-strict) global minimum point, as required.

$\square$

# 4

## Portfolios of multiple assets

Having developed the required mathematical tools, the tasks of finding the minimum variance portfolio, minimum variance line and market portfolio for portfolios of $n$ risky assets can be cast as constrained minimisation problems whose solutions are provided by applying the method of Lagrange multipliers. Using simple linear algebra, the formulae for the minimum variance and market portfolios and the capital market line can be shown to mirror those found for portfolios of two assets. The derivations of these formulae will be preceded by an examination of the portfolios of three assets in order to provide geometric intuition.

### 4.1 Risk and return

A portfolio constructed from $n$ different securities can be described by means of the vector of weights

$$\mathbf{w} = (w_1, \ldots, w_n),$$

with the constraint $\sum_{j=1}^{n} w_j = 1$. Denoting by $\mathbf{1}$ the $n$-dimensional vector

$$\mathbf{1} = (1, \ldots, 1),$$

the constraint can conveniently be written as

$$\mathbf{w}^{\mathrm{T}} \mathbf{1} = 1. \tag{4.1}$$

48

The **attainable set** is the set of all weight vectors $\mathbf{w}$ that satisfy this constraint.

If short-selling is not possible, the condition $w_j \geq 0$ is added to the constraint, so in that case the attainable set becomes

$$\{\mathbf{w} : \mathbf{w}^{\mathrm{T}}\mathbf{1} = 1, w_j \geq 0 \text{ for all } j \leq n\}.$$

Unless stated otherwise, we shall assume availability of short sales.

Alternatively a portfolio is described by the vector of positions taken in particular components (numbers of units of assets)

$$\mathbf{x} = (x_1, \ldots, x_n).$$

We have the following relations between the weights, prices and the numbers of shares:

$$w_j = \frac{x_j S_j(0)}{V(0)}, \quad j = 1, \ldots, n,$$

where $x_j$ is the number of shares of security $j$ in the portfolio, $S_j(0)$ is the initial price of security $j$, and $V(0)$ is the total money invested.

Denote the random returns on the securities by $K_1, \ldots, K_n$, and the vector of expected returns by

$$\boldsymbol{\mu} = (\mu_1, \ldots, \mu_n),$$

with

$$\mu_j = \mathbb{E}(K_j), \quad \text{for } j = 1, \ldots, n.$$

The covariances between returns will be denoted by $\sigma_{jk} = \mathrm{Cov}(K_j, K_k)$, in particular $\sigma_{jj} = \sigma_j^2 = \mathrm{Var}(K_j)$. These are the entries of the $n \times n$ **covariance matrix**

$$C = \begin{bmatrix} \sigma_{11} & \sigma_{12} & \cdots & \sigma_{1n} \\ \sigma_{21} & \sigma_{22} & \cdots & \sigma_{2n} \\ \vdots & \vdots & \ddots & \vdots \\ \sigma_{n1} & \sigma_{n2} & \cdots & \sigma_{nn} \end{bmatrix}.$$

---

**Exercise 4.1**  Assume that $C$ is invertible. Show that $C^{-1}$ is symmetric.

---

We write as before

$$K_{\mathbf{w}} = \sum_{j=1}^{n} w_j K_j.$$

Theorem 2.4 can easily be generalised.

**Theorem 4.1**
*The expected return $\mu_{\mathbf{w}} = \mathbb{E}(K_{\mathbf{w}})$ and variance $\sigma_{\mathbf{w}}^2 = \mathrm{Var}(K_{\mathbf{w}})$ of a portfolio with weights $\mathbf{w}$ are given by*

$$\mu_{\mathbf{w}} = \mathbf{w}^{\mathrm{T}}\boldsymbol{\mu},$$
$$\sigma_{\mathbf{w}}^2 = \mathbf{w}^{\mathrm{T}}C\mathbf{w}.$$

*Proof* The formula for $\mu_{\mathbf{w}}$ follows from the linearity of mathematical expectation:

$$\mu_{\mathbf{w}} = \mathbb{E}(K_{\mathbf{w}}) = \mathbb{E}\left(\sum_{j=1}^{n} w_j K_j\right) = \sum_{j=1}^{n} w_j \mathbb{E}(K_j) = \sum_{j=1}^{n} w_j \mu_j = \mathbf{w}^{\mathrm{T}}\boldsymbol{\mu}.$$

For $\sigma_{\mathbf{w}}^2$ we use the bilinearity of covariance:

$$\begin{aligned}
\sigma_{\mathbf{w}}^2 &= \mathrm{Var}(K_{\mathbf{w}}) \\
&= \mathrm{Cov}\,(K_{\mathbf{w}}, K_{\mathbf{w}}) \\
&= \mathrm{Cov}\left(\sum_{j=1}^{n} w_j K_j, \sum_{k=1}^{n} w_k K_k\right) \\
&= \sum_{j,k=1}^{n} w_j w_k \sigma_{jk} \qquad (\text{since } \mathrm{Cov}(K_j, K_k) = \sigma_{jk}) \\
&= \mathbf{w}^{\mathrm{T}}C\mathbf{w}.
\end{aligned}$$

□

---

**Exercise 4.2**   Show that the covariance matrix is symmetric and positive semidefinite. (Recall that $C$ is positive semidefinite if for any $\mathbf{x} \in \mathbb{R}^n$, $\mathbf{x}^{\mathrm{T}}C\mathbf{x} \geq 0$.) Does $C$ have to be invertible?

---

**Exercise 4.3**   Show that any invertible covariance matrix $C$ is positive definite. (We say that $C$ is positive definite if for any $\mathbf{x} \in \mathbb{R}^n$, $\mathbf{x} \neq \mathbf{0}$, $\mathbf{x}^{\mathrm{T}}C\mathbf{x} > 0$.)

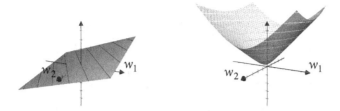

**Figure 4.1** The plots of $\mu_{\mathbf{w}}$ and $\sigma_{\mathbf{w}}$ with respect to $w_1, w_2$.

**Exercise 4.4** Investigate the limit behaviour of the sequence $\sigma_{\mathbf{w}}$ as $n \to \infty$, taking $w_j = \frac{1}{n}$. Formulate sufficient conditions for $\sigma_{\mathbf{w}}$ to be convergent.

**Proposition 4.2**

*For any two portfolios*

$$\mathbf{w}_A = (w_{A,1}, \ldots, w_{A,n}),$$
$$\mathbf{w}_B = (w_{B,1}, \ldots, w_{B,n}),$$

*the covariance between the returns is*

$$\mathrm{Cov}(K_{\mathbf{w}_A}, K_{\mathbf{w}_B}) = \mathbf{w}_A^{\mathrm{T}} C \mathbf{w}_B.$$

*Proof*   Using the bilinearity of covariance we compute

$$
\begin{aligned}
\mathrm{Cov}(K_{\mathbf{w}_A}, K_{\mathbf{w}_B}) &= \mathrm{Cov}\left(\sum_{j=1}^{n} w_{A,j} K_j, \sum_{k=1}^{n} w_{B,k} K_k\right) \\
&= \sum_{j,k=1}^{n} w_{A,j} w_{B,k} \sigma_{jk} \qquad (\text{since } \mathrm{Cov}(K_j, K_k) = \sigma_{jk}) \\
&= \mathbf{w}_A^{\mathrm{T}} C \mathbf{w}_B,
\end{aligned}
$$

as required. □

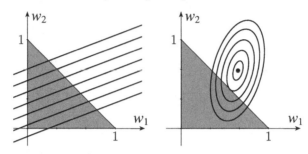

**Figure 4.2** The lines $\mu_{\mathbf{w}} = m$ (left) and the curves $\sigma_{\mathbf{w}} = c$ (right).

## 4.2  Three risky securities

The purpose of this section is to provide geometric intuition as to the shape of the attainable set.

In the case when we have three risky assets, the third weight of a portfolio can be computed from the first two weights

$$w_3 = 1 - w_2 - w_1,$$

meaning that the attainable set is parameterised by $w_1$ and $w_2$. We can write the formulae for $\mu_{\mathbf{w}}$ and $\sigma_{\mathbf{w}}$ with respect to these two parameters as

$$\mu_{\mathbf{w}} = w_1\mu_1 + w_2\mu_2 + w_3\mu_3$$
$$= w_1\mu_1 + w_2\mu_2 + (1 - w_1 - w_2)\mu_3,$$

and

$$\sigma_{\mathbf{w}}^2 = w_1^2\sigma_1^2 + w_2^2\sigma_2^2 + w_3^2\sigma_3^2 + 2w_1w_2\sigma_{12} + 2w_1w_3\sigma_{13} + 2w_2w_3\sigma_{23}$$
$$= w_1^2\sigma_1^2 + w_2^2\sigma_2^2 + (1 - w_2 - w_1)^2 \sigma_3^2 + 2w_1w_2\sigma_{12}$$
$$+2w_1 (1 - w_2 - w_1)\sigma_{13} + 2w_2 (1 - w_2 - w_1)\sigma_{23}.$$

The plots of $\mu_{\mathbf{w}}$ and $\sigma_{\mathbf{w}}$ are given in Figure 4.1. The lines on the graphs represent the level sets $\{\mu_{\mathbf{w}} = m\}$ and $\{\sigma_{\mathbf{w}} = c\}$ for several values of $m$ and $c$.

Since the third weight can be computed from the first two, the attainable set is represented as the $(w_1, w_2)$-plane in Figure 4.2. The vertices of the grey triangle represent investments in single assets. The point $(1, 0)$ represents the first asset, $(0, 1)$ the second asset, and since $w_3 = 1 - w_1 - w_2$, the point $(0, 0)$ represents the third asset. The grey triangle consists of the points

$$\{(w_1, w_2)\,|\,w_1, w_2 \geq 0, w_1 + w_2 \leq 1\}, \tag{4.2}$$

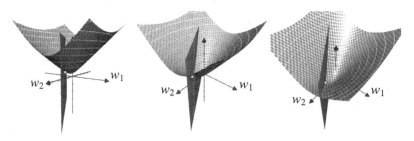

**Figure 4.3** The plot of $\sigma_\mathbf{w}$ together with $\mu_\mathbf{w} = m$.

and contains portfolios attainable without short-selling.

The level sets $\{\mu_\mathbf{w} = m\}$ and $\{\sigma_\mathbf{w} = c\}$ from Figure 4.1 can be projected onto the $(w_1, w_2)$-plane in Figure 4.2. These are the straight lines and ellipses in Figure 4.2, respectively. The middle point of the ellipses is the minimum variance portfolio. In this particular figure, since the point lies outside of the triangle, we see that the minimum variance portfolio requires short selling. In Figure 4.2 we also see that if short-selling is not allowed, then the smallest attainable $\sigma_\mathbf{w}$ lies on the ellipse which is tangent to the grey triangle. The minimum variance portfolio without short-selling is the tangency point.

We now discuss the shape that the set of attainable portfolios takes in the $(\sigma, \mu)$-plane. We start with Figure 4.3, where we see the plane corresponding to portfolios with $\mu_\mathbf{w} = m$, together with the plot of $\sigma_\mathbf{w}$. We see that there is a single point that has smallest attainable variance under the constraint $\mu_\mathbf{w} = m$. This is the point at the bottom of the intersection of the plane with the hyperbola. From the plot we also see that for $\mu_\mathbf{w} = m$ we can have portfolios with arbitrarily large $\sigma$. This leads to the conclusion that in the $(\sigma, \mu)$-plane, the set of portfolios with $\mu_\mathbf{w} = m$ is a horizontal half line, which is depicted in Figure 4.4. Intuitively one can think of Figure 4.4 as the leftmost graph from Figure 4.3, rotated clockwise by ninety degrees, and projected onto the plane. Since the plot of $\sigma_\mathbf{w}$ is a hyperbola, one is led to believe that the boundary of the attainable set on the $(\sigma, \mu)$-plane should also be a hyperbola. This is just a geometric intuition, and is by no means meant as a proof. We shall prove this fact later on.

When short-selling is not allowed, the attainable set is restricted to the set from (4.2). In that case, in the $(\sigma, \mu)$-plane the attainable set takes the shape depicted in Figure 4.5. The three points represent the three assets. A hyperbola passing through any two points represents portfolios involving

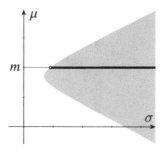

**Figure 4.4**  Attainable portfolios.

investments in the two securities corresponding to the points. The fragments of the hyperbolas between two points correspond to the edges of the triangle from Figure 4.2. The attainable set in Figure 4.5 can therefore be interpreted as a distorted and folded projection of the triangle from Figure 4.2.

## 4.3  Minimum variance portfolio

In this section we give the formula for the weights of the portfolio with smallest variance. Before doing so, we need to consider a technical lemma.

**Lemma 4.3**
*We have the following formulae for the gradients computed with respect to* $\mathbf{w}$:

$$\nabla\left(\mathbf{w}^{\mathrm{T}}\mu\right) = \mu, \tag{4.3}$$

$$\nabla\left(\mathbf{w}^{\mathrm{T}}\mathbf{1}\right) = \mathbf{1}, \tag{4.4}$$

$$\nabla\left(\mathbf{w}^{\mathrm{T}}C\mathbf{w}\right) = 2C\mathbf{w}, \tag{4.5}$$

*and the Hessian of* $\mathbf{w}^{\mathrm{T}}C\mathbf{w}$ *is equal to* $2C$.

*Proof*  Since

$$\frac{\partial}{\partial w_i}\left(\mathbf{w}^{\mathrm{T}}\mu\right) = \frac{\partial}{\partial w_i}\left(w_1\mu_1 + \cdots + w_n\mu_n\right) = \mu_i$$

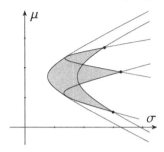

**Figure 4.5** Attainable portfolios with short-selling constraints.

we see that

$$\nabla\left(\mathbf{w}^{\mathrm{T}}\boldsymbol{\mu}\right) = \begin{bmatrix} \frac{\partial}{\partial w_1}\left(\mathbf{w}^{\mathrm{T}}\boldsymbol{\mu}\right) \\ \vdots \\ \frac{\partial}{\partial w_n}\left(\mathbf{w}^{\mathrm{T}}\boldsymbol{\mu}\right) \end{bmatrix} = \begin{bmatrix} \mu_1 \\ \vdots \\ \mu_n \end{bmatrix} = \boldsymbol{\mu},$$

which proves (4.3).

The proof of (4.4) follows from an identical argument, using $\mathbf{1}$ instead of $\boldsymbol{\mu}$.

To prove (4.5) we observe that in

$$\frac{\partial}{\partial w_i}\left(\mathbf{w}^{\mathrm{T}}C\mathbf{w}\right) = \frac{\partial}{\partial w_i}\sum_{j=1}^{n}\sum_{k=1}^{n}w_jw_k\sigma_{jk}$$

the derivative of each term can be non-zero only when $j = i$ or $k = i$. This means that

$$\frac{\partial}{\partial w_i}\sum_{j=1}^{n}\sum_{k=1}^{n}w_jw_k\sigma_{jk}$$

$$= \frac{\partial}{\partial w_i}\left(w_iw_i\sigma_{ii} + \sum_{j=i}\sum_{k\neq i}w_jw_k\sigma_{jk} + \sum_{j\neq i}\sum_{k=i}w_jw_k\sigma_{jk}\right)$$

$$= 2w_i\sigma_{ii} + \sum_{k\neq i}w_k\sigma_{ik} + \sum_{j\neq i}w_j\sigma_{ji}$$

$$= 2\sum_{k=1}^{n}w_k\sigma_{ik} \qquad \text{(since } \sigma_{ji} = \sigma_{ij}\text{)} \qquad (4.6)$$

$$= 2\left(C\mathbf{w}\right)_i$$

where $(C\mathbf{w})_i$ stands for the $i$-th coordinate of the vector $C\mathbf{w}$. Combining the partial derivatives on all coordinates gives (4.5).

Using (4.6) we can compute

$$\frac{\partial}{\partial w_l}\frac{\partial}{\partial w_i}\left(\mathbf{w}^\mathrm{T}C\mathbf{w}\right) = \frac{\partial}{\partial w_l}\left(2\sum_{k-1}^{n}w_k\sigma_{ik}\right)$$

$$= 2\sigma_{il}$$

$$= 2\sigma_{li},$$

hence

$$\left(\frac{\partial^2}{\partial w_l\partial w_i}\left(\mathbf{w}^\mathrm{T}C\mathbf{w}\right)\right)_{l,i\leq n} = (2\sigma_{li})_{l,i\leq n} = 2C,$$

which is the Hessian of $\mathbf{w}^\mathrm{T}C\mathbf{w}$ □

We are ready to derive the formula for the weights of the minimum variance portfolio.

**Theorem 4.4**
*The portfolio with the smallest variance in the attainable set has weights*

$$\mathbf{w}_{\min} = \frac{C^{-1}\mathbf{1}}{\mathbf{1}^\mathrm{T}C^{-1}\mathbf{1}}. \tag{4.7}$$

*Proof* We need to find the minimum of $\mathbf{w}^\mathrm{T}C\mathbf{w}$ subject to the constraint

$$\mathbf{w}^\mathrm{T}\mathbf{1} = 1. \tag{4.8}$$

To this end we use the method of Lagrange multipliers taking the Lagrangian

$$L(\mathbf{w}) = \nabla\left(\mathbf{w}^\mathrm{T}C\mathbf{w}\right) - \nabla\left(\lambda(\mathbf{1}^\mathrm{T}\mathbf{w} - 1)\right).$$

By (4.4) and (4.5) from Lemma 4.3,

$$L(\mathbf{w}) = 2C\mathbf{w} - \lambda\mathbf{1} = 0,$$

hence

$$\mathbf{w} = \frac{\lambda}{2}C^{-1}\mathbf{1}. \tag{4.9}$$

Substituting this into the constraint (4.8), we obtain

$$1 = \mathbf{w}^\mathrm{T}\mathbf{1} = \mathbf{1}^\mathrm{T}\mathbf{w} = \frac{\lambda}{2}\mathbf{1}^\mathrm{T}C^{-1}\mathbf{1}.$$

Solving this for $\lambda$ and substituting the result into (4.9) gives (4.7). We have shown that (4.7) is the only candidate for a local extremum. From Lemma 4.3 we know that the Hessian of $\mathbf{w}^\mathrm{T}C\mathbf{w}$ is $2C$, which is positive semidefinite. By Theorem 3.4 this means that $\mathbf{w}_{\min}$ is a global minimum. □

The minimum variance portfolio has the surprising property that its co-variance with any other portfolio is constant. This property will prove useful later on, when discussing the shape of the attainable set in the $(\sigma, \mu)$-plane.

**Corollary 4.5**
*For any portfolio* $\mathbf{w}$

$$\mathrm{Cov}(K_{\mathbf{w}}, K_{\mathbf{w}_{\min}}) = \sigma^2_{\mathbf{w}_{\min}}.$$

*Proof* By Proposition 4.2

$$\begin{aligned}
\mathrm{Cov}(K_{\mathbf{w}}, K_{\mathbf{w}_{\min}}) &= \mathbf{w}^{\mathrm{T}} C \mathbf{w}_{\min} \\
&= \mathbf{w}^{\mathrm{T}} C \frac{C^{-1}\mathbf{1}}{\mathbf{1}^{\mathrm{T}} C^{-1}\mathbf{1}} \\
&= \frac{\mathbf{w}^{\mathrm{T}}\mathbf{1}}{\mathbf{1}^{\mathrm{T}} C^{-1}\mathbf{1}} \\
&= \frac{1}{\mathbf{1}^{\mathrm{T}} C^{-1}\mathbf{1}}. \quad (4.10)
\end{aligned}$$

The above holds for any portfolio $\mathbf{w}$, hence also in particular for $\mathbf{w} = \mathbf{w}_{\min}$, giving

$$\sigma^2_{\mathbf{w}_{\min}} = \mathrm{Var}(K_{\mathbf{w}_{\min}}) = \mathrm{Cov}(K_{\mathbf{w}_{\min}}, K_{\mathbf{w}_{\min}}) = \frac{1}{\mathbf{1}^{\mathrm{T}} C^{-1}\mathbf{1}}. \quad (4.11)$$

Combining (4.10) with (4.11) we obtain our claim. □

## 4.4 Minimum variance line

To find the efficient frontier, we have to recognise and eliminate the dominated portfolios. To this end we fix a level of expected return, denote it by $m$, and consider all portfolios with $\mu_{\mathbf{w}} = m$. All of these are redundant except the one with the smallest variance. The family of such portfolios, parameterised by $m$, is called the **minimum variance line** (see Figure 4.6).

More precisely, portfolios on the minimum variance line are solutions of the following problem:

$$\begin{aligned}
\min \; &\mathbf{w}^{\mathrm{T}} C \mathbf{w}, \\
\text{subject to:} \quad &\mathbf{w}^{\mathrm{T}} \mu = m, \quad (4.12) \\
&\mathbf{w}^{\mathrm{T}} \mathbf{1} = 1.
\end{aligned}$$

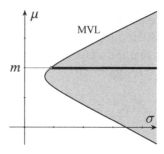

**Figure 4.6** Minimum variance line (MVL).

**Theorem 4.6**
*Let M be a $2 \times 2$ matrix of the form*

$$M = \begin{bmatrix} \mu^T C^{-1} \mu & \mu^T C^{-1} \mathbf{1} \\ \mu^T C^{-1} \mathbf{1} & \mathbf{1}^T C^{-1} \mathbf{1} \end{bmatrix}.$$

*If C and M are invertible, then the solution of problem (4.12) is given by*

$$\mathbf{w} = \frac{1}{\det(M)} C^{-1} \left( \det(M_1) \mu + \det(M_2) \mathbf{1} \right), \tag{4.13}$$

*where*

$$M_1 = \begin{bmatrix} m & \mu^T C^{-1} \mathbf{1} \\ 1 & \mathbf{1}^T C^{-1} \mathbf{1} \end{bmatrix}, \qquad M_2 = \begin{bmatrix} \mu^T C^{-1} \mu & m \\ \mu^T C^{-1} \mathbf{1} & 1 \end{bmatrix}.$$

*Proof* We introduce the Lagrange multiplier $\lambda = (\lambda_1, \lambda_2)$, and the Lagrangian

$$L(\mathbf{w}) = \nabla \left( \mathbf{w}^T C \mathbf{w} \right) - \lambda_1 \nabla \left( \mathbf{w}^T \mu - m \right) + \lambda_2 \nabla \left( \mathbf{w}^T \mathbf{1} - 1 \right) = 0.$$

Using Lemma 4.3 we can compute

$$L(\mathbf{w}) = 2C\mathbf{w} - \lambda_1 \mu - \lambda_2 \mathbf{1} = 0.$$

We solve this system for $\mathbf{w}$:

$$\mathbf{w} = \frac{1}{2} \lambda_1 C^{-1} \mu + \frac{1}{2} \lambda_2 C^{-1} \mathbf{1}. \tag{4.14}$$

Since $\mathbf{w}^T \mu = \mu^T \mathbf{w}$ and $\mathbf{w}^T \mathbf{1} = \mathbf{1}^T \mathbf{w}$, substituting (4.14) into the constraints from (4.12), we obtain a system of linear equations

$$\frac{1}{2} \lambda_1 \mu^T C^{-1} \mu + \frac{1}{2} \lambda_2 \mu^T C^{-1} \mathbf{1} = m,$$

$$\frac{1}{2} \lambda_1 \mathbf{1}^T C^{-1} \mu + \frac{1}{2} \lambda_2 \mathbf{1}^T C^{-1} \mathbf{1} = 1.$$

We can solve the above system for $\lambda_1$ and $\lambda_2$ to obtain (note the relevance of the assumption that $M$ is invertible, which ensures that $\det(M) \neq 0$)

$$\frac{1}{2}\lambda_1 = \frac{\det(M_1)}{\det(M)}, \qquad \frac{1}{2}\lambda_2 = \frac{\det(M_2)}{\det(M)}.$$

Substituting the above back into (4.14) gives (4.13).

We have found a candidate for the solution of (4.12). By Lemma 4.3 we know that the Hessian of $\mathbf{w}^T C \mathbf{w}$ is equal $2C$, which is a positive semidefinite matrix. By Theorem 3.4 this ensures that we have found a global minimum. $\qquad\square$

---

**Exercise 4.5** Consider three uncorrelated assets with

$$\begin{array}{ccc} \sigma_1^2 = 0.01, & \sigma_2^2 = 0.02, & \sigma_3^2 = 0.04, \\ \mu_1 = 10\%, & \mu_2 = 20\%, & \mu_3 = 30\%. \end{array}$$

Using (4.13) compute the portfolio which solves the problem (4.12) for $m = 25\%$.

---

The formula (4.13) is long and somewhat cumbersome to apply. Our aim will be to simplify it. The first step towards this end is to notice that all portfolios on the minimum variance line can be expressed by means of an affine function of $m$ involving two fixed vectors.

**Corollary 4.7**
*There exist two vectors **a** and **b**, which depend only on $C$ and $\mu$, such that for any real m the solution of the problem (4.12) is*

$$\mathbf{w} = m\mathbf{a} + \mathbf{b}.$$

*Proof* Since

$$\det(M_1) = m\mathbf{1}^T C^{-1} \mathbf{1} - \mu^T C^{-1} \mathbf{1},$$
$$\det(M_2) = \mu^T C^{-1} \mu - m\mu^T C^{-1} \mathbf{1},$$

from (4.13) we see that $\mathbf{w} = m\mathbf{a} + \mathbf{b}$ for

$$\mathbf{a} = \frac{1}{\det(M)} C^{-1} \left( \left( \mathbf{1}^T C^{-1} \mathbf{1} \right) \mu - \left( \mu^T C^{-1} \mathbf{1} \right) \mathbf{1} \right),$$

$$\mathbf{b} = \frac{1}{\det(M)} C^{-1} \left( \left( \mu^T C^{-1} \mu \right) \mathbf{1} - \left( \mu^T C^{-1} \mathbf{1} \right) \mu \right).$$

$\qquad\square$

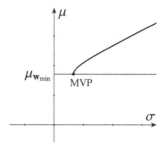

**Figure 4.7** Efficient frontier, together with the minimum variance portfolio (MVP).

The efficient frontier, which is the set of all portfolios not dominated by any other portfolios, consists of $\mathbf{w} = \mathbf{a}m + \mathbf{b}$ for $m \geq \mu_{\mathbf{w}_{\min}}$ (see Figure 4.7).

We now show that the whole minimum variance line can be found from just two portfolios. This result is often referred to as the **two-fund theorem**, since it means that two efficient portfolios (with unequal returns) suffice to establish an efficient investment policy.

**Corollary 4.8**
*Suppose that $\mathbf{w}_1$ and $\mathbf{w}_2$ are two portfolios on the minimum variance line with different expected returns: $\mu_{\mathbf{w}_1} \neq \mu_{\mathbf{w}_2}$. Then any portfolio $\mathbf{w}$ on the minimum variance line can be obtained from these two, that is, there is a real number $\alpha$ such that $\mathbf{w} = \alpha\mathbf{w}_1 + (1 - \alpha)\mathbf{w}_2$.*

*Proof* We first find $\alpha$ so that

$$\mu_{\mathbf{w}} = \alpha\mu_{\mathbf{w}_1} + (1 - \alpha)\mu_{\mathbf{w}_2}.$$

This is possible since the returns are different:

$$\alpha = \frac{\mu_{\mathbf{w}} - \mu_{\mathbf{w}_2}}{\mu_{\mathbf{w}_1} - \mu_{\mathbf{w}_2}}.$$

Since the two portfolios lie on the minimum variance line, they satisfy

$$\mathbf{w}_1 = \mu_{\mathbf{w}_1}\mathbf{a} + \mathbf{b},$$
$$\mathbf{w}_2 = \mu_{\mathbf{w}_2}\mathbf{a} + \mathbf{b}.$$

From these relations we have

$$\alpha\mathbf{w}_1 + (1 - \alpha)\mathbf{w}_2 = (\alpha\mu_{\mathbf{w}_1} + (1 - \alpha)\mu_{\mathbf{w}_2})\mathbf{a} + \mathbf{b} = \mu_{\mathbf{w}}\mathbf{a} + \mathbf{b},$$

but $\mathbf{w}$ is also on the minimum variance line so $\mathbf{w} = \mu_{\mathbf{w}}\mathbf{a} + \mathbf{b}$, hence the result.                                                                  □

The minimum variance portfolio $\mathbf{w}_{\min}$ lies on the minimum variance line. We therefore already have a simple formula (4.7) for one of the two portfolios needed to obtain the minimum variance line. The second portfolio is the market portfolio, whose formula will be derived in the next section. The resulting parameterisation of the minimum variance line will then be written out in equation (4.18).

From Corollary 4.8 we obtain the following important observation.

**Theorem 4.9**
*Suppose that there exist two portfolios $\mathbf{w}_1$ and $\mathbf{w}_2$ on the minimum variance line with different expected returns: $\mu_{\mathbf{w}_1} \neq \mu_{\mathbf{w}_2}$. Then the minimum variance line is a hyperbola centred on the vertical axis.*

*Proof* Let $K_{\mathbf{w}_1}$ and $K_{\mathbf{w}_2}$ be the returns on portfolios $\mathbf{w}_1$ and $\mathbf{w}_2$, respectively. From Corollary 4.8 we know that any portfolio on the minimum variance line can be expressed as

$$\mathbf{w} = \alpha \mathbf{w}_1 + (1 - \alpha)\mathbf{w}_2,$$

hence its return is equal to

$$K_{\mathbf{w}} = \alpha K_{\mathbf{w}_1} + (1 - \alpha)K_{\mathbf{w}_2}.$$

We can treat each of the two portfolios as if it were a single security. Applying the results from Chapter 2 for portfolios consisting of two securities, we know that

$$\mu_{\mathbf{w}} = \alpha \mu_{\mathbf{w}_1} + (1 - \alpha)\mu_{\mathbf{w}_2},$$
$$\sigma_{\mathbf{w}}^2 = \alpha^2 \sigma_{\mathbf{w}_1}^2 + (1 - \alpha)^2 \sigma_{\mathbf{w}_2}^2 + 2\alpha(1 - \alpha)\operatorname{Cov}(K_{\mathbf{w}_1}, K_{\mathbf{w}_2}).$$

Since $\mu_{\mathbf{w}_1} \neq \mu_{\mathbf{w}_2}$, by Theorem 2.7 the curve $(\sigma_{\mathbf{w}}, \mu_{\mathbf{w}})$ is a hyperbola. $\square$

---

**Exercise 4.6** Consider three securities with the following parameters:

$$C = \begin{bmatrix} 0.01 & 0 & 0 \\ 0 & 0.02 & 0.02 \\ 0 & 0.02 & 0.04 \end{bmatrix}, \quad \mu = \begin{pmatrix} 0.1 \\ 0.2 \\ 0.3 \end{pmatrix}.$$

Find the vectors **a**, **b** described in Corollary (4.7). Using **a** and **b** compute the vector on the minimum variance line corresponding to $m = 20\%$.

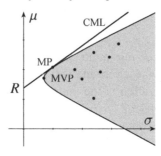

**Figure 4.8** Minimum variance portfolio (MVP), the market portfolio (MP), and the capital market line (CML).

**Exercise 4.7** Consider the data from Exercise 4.6. Plot the minimum variance line in the $(w_1, w_2)$-plane. Consider two portfolios corresponding to $m = 10\%$ and $m = 20\%$. Find the variances of, as well as the covariance between, their returns. Use these to plot the minimum variance line in the $(\sigma, \mu)$ plane.

**Exercise 4.8** Consider the data from Exercise 4.6. Find the weights and the expected return of a portfolio on the minimum variance line with $\sigma^2 = 0.007$.

## 4.5 Market portfolio

Recall that the market portfolio is the optimal portfolio on the efficient frontier taking into account the existence of a risk-free asset. The line connecting the market portfolio with the risk-free asset is tangent to the minimum variance line and has maximal slope among the lines determined by all portfolios (see Figure 4.8).

In Chapter 2 we found the formula for the market portfolio obtained in the case of two risky securities determining the efficient set. This result is of course applicable to the general situation in view of Corollary 4.8.

However, we derive the formula again; this time the parameters of all $n$ securities will be used.

**Theorem 4.10**
*If the risk-free return $R$ is smaller than the expected return of the minimum variance portfolio, then the market portfolio exists and is given by*

$$\mathbf{m} = \frac{C^{-1}(\mu - R\mathbf{1})}{\mathbf{1}^{\mathrm{T}}C^{-1}(\mu - R\mathbf{1})}. \tag{4.15}$$

*Proof* From Theorem 4.9 we know that the minimum variance line is a hyperbola. Since its centre is on the vertical axis, there exists a single tangency point for a half line emanating from $(0, R)$, which maximises the slope (see Figure 4.8). The slope in question is of the form

$$\frac{\mu_{\mathbf{w}} - R}{\sigma_{\mathbf{w}}} = \frac{\mathbf{w}^{\mathrm{T}}\mu - R}{\sqrt{\mathbf{w}^{\mathrm{T}}C\mathbf{w}}},$$

where $\mathbf{w}$ are the weights of a portfolio and $R$ is the risk-free rate of return. At the maximal slope the Lagrangian

$$L(\mathbf{w}) = \nabla\left(\frac{\mathbf{w}^{\mathrm{T}}\mu - R}{\sqrt{\mathbf{w}^{\mathrm{T}}C\mathbf{w}}}\right) - \lambda\nabla(\mathbf{w}^{\mathrm{T}}\mathbf{1} - 1),$$

needs to be equal to zero. We can compute the gradients using Lemma 4.3 and equate them to zero:

$$L(\mathbf{w}) = \frac{\mu\sqrt{\mathbf{w}^{\mathrm{T}}C\mathbf{w}} - (\mathbf{w}^{\mathrm{T}}\mu - R)\frac{1}{2\sqrt{\mathbf{w}^{\mathrm{T}}C\mathbf{w}}}2C\mathbf{w}}{\mathbf{w}^{\mathrm{T}}C\mathbf{w}} - \lambda\mathbf{1} = \mathbf{0}.$$

This yields

$$\mu\sigma_{\mathbf{w}} - (\mu_{\mathbf{w}} - R)\frac{C\mathbf{w}}{\sigma_{\mathbf{w}}} - \lambda\sigma_{\mathbf{w}}^2\mathbf{1} = \mathbf{0},$$

hence

$$\frac{\mu_{\mathbf{w}} - R}{\sigma_{\mathbf{w}}^2}C\mathbf{w} = \mu - \lambda\sigma_{\mathbf{w}}\mathbf{1}.$$

Multiplying by $\mathbf{w}^{\mathrm{T}}$ on the left and using the fact that $\mathbf{w}^{\mathrm{T}}\mathbf{1} = 1$ we get

$$\frac{\mu_{\mathbf{w}} - R}{\sigma_{\mathbf{w}}^2}\mathbf{w}^{\mathrm{T}}C\mathbf{w} = \mu_{\mathbf{w}} - \lambda\sigma_{\mathbf{w}},$$

so

$$\lambda = \frac{R}{\sigma_{\mathbf{w}}},$$

therefore we have the equation

$$\gamma C \mathbf{w} = \mu - R\mathbf{1},$$

where $\gamma = \frac{\mu_{\mathbf{w}} - R}{\sigma_{\mathbf{w}}^2}$. Therefore

$$\gamma \mathbf{w} = C^{-1}(\mu - R\mathbf{1}). \tag{4.16}$$

Even though we have $\mathbf{w}$ in the formula for $\gamma$, we show that $\gamma$ turns out to be a constant. This follows from multiplying the above equation by $\mathbf{1}^{\mathrm{T}}$ on both sides, which gives

$$\gamma = \mathbf{1}^{\mathrm{T}} C^{-1}(\mu - R\mathbf{1}).$$

By substituting $\gamma$ into (4.16) we obtain our claim.                                    □

---

**Exercise 4.9**    Prove that when $R$ is equal to the expected return of the minimum variance portfolio, then the formula for the market portfolio results in a division by zero. Explain geometrically why this is so.

---

The line joining the risk-free security represented by $(0, R)$ and the market portfolio with coordinates $(\sigma_{\mathbf{m}}, \mu_{\mathbf{m}})$ is given by the equation

$$\mu = R + \frac{\mu_{\mathbf{m}} - R}{\sigma_{\mathbf{m}}} \sigma. \tag{4.17}$$

It is called the **capital market line**, CML in brief. For a portfolio on CML with risk $\sigma$ the term $\frac{\mu_{\mathbf{m}} - R}{\sigma_{\mathbf{m}}} \sigma$ is called the **risk premium**, which is the additional return above the risk-free level, representing a reward or compensation for exposure to risk.

If all the investors agree on the values of the model parameters (the expected returns on the basic assets and the entries of the covariance matrix) and if each investor chooses an optimal portfolio according to convex indifference curves on the basis of risk-return analysis, then all these optimal portfolios are placed on the CML. Consequently, they should all invest in just one risky portfolio, namely the market portfolio (combining it with the risk-free asset in a preferred individual way). Consequently, the market portfolio weights should represent the relative volumes of the values of particular shares of stock with respect to the whole market (just as in Chapter 2, where we discussed a simple market with just two ingredients). Such a portfolio is represented in practice by the market index.

We now return to our discussion of the shape of the minimum variance line. From Corollary 4.8 we know that this line can be constructed using

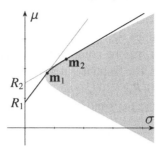

**Figure 4.9** Efficient frontier in the case of different rates for investing and borrowing risk free.

$\mathbf{w}_{min}$ and $\mathbf{m}$. By Corollary 4.8, $\text{Cov}(K_{\mathbf{w}_{min}}, K_{\mathbf{m}}) = \sigma^2_{\mathbf{w}_{min}}$, which gives the following parameterisation of all $(\sigma_{\mathbf{w}}, \mu_{\mathbf{w}})$ on the minimum variance line:

$$\mu_{\mathbf{w}} = \alpha\mu_{\mathbf{w}_{min}} + (1 - \alpha)\mu_{\mathbf{m}}, \tag{4.18}$$
$$\sigma^2_{\mathbf{w}} = \alpha^2\sigma^2_{\mathbf{w}_{min}} + (1 - \alpha)^2\sigma^2_{\mathbf{m}} + 2\alpha(1 - \alpha)\sigma^2_{\mathbf{w}_{min}}.$$

The quantities $\mu_{\mathbf{w}_{min}}, \sigma_{\mathbf{w}_{min}}, \mu_{\mathbf{m}}$ and $\sigma_{\mathbf{m}}$ are easy to compute, due to the simplicity of the expressions for $\mathbf{w}_{min}$ and $\mathbf{m}$ (see (4.7) and (4.15)). This makes (4.18) a handy tool for making plots of the minimum variance line.

We conclude this chapter by considering a situation where we have different rates for risk-free borrowing and investing. This is a more realistic setting than assuming that we have a single risk-free rate of return $R$.

Assume that we can invest risk-free at a rate of return $R_1$ and borrow at $R_2$. We assume that $R_1 < R_2$, since the opposite inequality would allow investors to make risk-free profits. Any portfolio $\mathbf{w}$ invested in the risky securities can be combined with a risk-free investment at the rate of return $R_1$. This gives the following portfolios on the $(\sigma, \mu)$-plane:

$$\begin{aligned} \mu_{\alpha} &= \alpha R_1 + (1 - \alpha)\mu_{\mathbf{w}}, \\ \sigma_{\alpha} &= |1 - \alpha|\sigma_{\mathbf{w}}, \end{aligned} \qquad \text{for } \alpha \geq 0.$$

Note that we can not take $\alpha < 0$, since this implies a short position at $R_1$, which would mean borrowing at $R_1$.

We can also combine any portfolio $\mathbf{w}$ with borrowing at $R_2$, giving

$$\begin{aligned} \mu_{\alpha} &= \alpha R_2 + (1 - \alpha)\mu_{\mathbf{w}}, \\ \sigma_{\alpha} &= (1 - \alpha)\sigma_{\mathbf{w}}, \end{aligned} \qquad \text{for } \alpha \leq 0.$$

We cannot take $\alpha > 0$ here since this would mean investing at $R_2$, which is not allowed. We can only borrow at this rate.

To find the efficient frontier we first establish two tangency portfolios $\mathbf{m}_1$ and $\mathbf{m}_2$, for the half-lines starting from $(0, R_1)$ and $(0, R_2)$, respectively. The portfolios $\mathbf{m}_1$ and $\mathbf{m}_2$ can be computed using (4.15) taking $R_1$ and $R_2$ instead of $R$, respectively. The frontier is depicted in Figure 4.9 and consists of the interval between $(0, R_1)$ to $(\sigma_{\mathbf{m}_1}, \mu_{\mathbf{m}_1})$, the fragment of the minimum variance line between $(\sigma_{\mathbf{m}_1}, \mu_{\mathbf{m}_1})$ and $(\sigma_{\mathbf{m}_2}, \mu_{\mathbf{m}_2})$, together with the half line starting from $(\sigma_{\mathbf{m}_2}, \mu_{\mathbf{m}_2})$.

---

**Exercise 4.10**   Consider the data from Exercise 4.6. Let $R_1 = 5\%$ and $R_2 = 10\%$. Assume that we invest $V = 1000$. Determine how we should divide $V$ amongst the securities to obtain an efficient portfolio with:

(i) $\sigma^2 = 0.003$;

(ii) $\sigma^2 = 0.023$;

(iii) $\sigma^2 = 0.16$.

# 5

## The Capital Asset Pricing Model

The market portfolio exists when the return on the minimum variance portfolio exceeds the risk-free return. The Capital Asset Pricing Model (CAPM) provides a linear relationship between the expected return $\mu_m$ on the market portfolio and that of any risky asset. The two are linked by means of a parameter, commonly known as the beta ($\beta$), providing a measure of undiversifiable risk of an asset. In the chapter we explore this relationship and show how the CAPM formula can assist investment decisions and introduce measures of portfolio performance.

Paradoxically, although we use variance to quantify risk, in assessing portfolio risk the variances of the assets in the portfolio turn out to be less relevant than their mutual covariances. To demonstrate this, let us consider the following example.

### Example 5.1

Suppose that the weights of a portfolio are of the form $w_j = \frac{1}{n}$, $j \leq n$, where $n$ is the number of assets in the portfolio. We investigate the risk of this portfolio in terms of its dependence on $n$. Assume that the variances of all securities on the market are uniformly bounded, $\sigma_j^2 \leq L$. Then

$$\sigma_w^2 = \sum_{j,k=1}^{n} w_j w_k \sigma_{jk} = \sum_{j=1}^{n} w_j^2 \sigma_j^2 + \sum_{j \neq k} w_j w_k \sigma_{jk} \leq n\frac{1}{n^2}L + \frac{1}{n^2}\sum_{j \neq k} \sigma_{jk}.$$

Assume further that the off-diagonal elements of the covariance matrix are uniformly bounded, $|\sigma_{jk}| \leq c$, for some $c > 0$. Then

$$\sigma_w^2 \leq \frac{L}{n} + \frac{1}{n^2} n(n-1)c.$$

The upper bound converges to $c$ as $n \to \infty$. Hence the risk of a portfolio containing many assets is determined by the covariances. The variances of the ingredients become irrelevant for large $n$.

This example motivates the following distinction between two kinds of risk: **diversifiable**, or **specific risk,** which can be reduced to zero by expanding the portfolio, and **undiversifiable, systematic,** or **market risk,** which cannot be avoided because the securities are linked to the market

From the above example we see that the variances of returns on individual securities are not the leading factors in determining the risk of a portfolio. The risk should rather depend on its undiversifiable risk, which should in turn depend on the asset's covariances with the remaining assets. The aim of the Capital Asset Pricing Model (CAPM) is to quantify the systematic risk of an asset and to link it with its expected return.

## 5.1   Derivation of CAPM

In this section we derive the Capital Asset Pricing Model formula for the expected return of a risky security. Before doing so we need the following definition.

**Definition 5.2**
We call

$$\beta_i = \frac{\text{Cov}(K_i, K_m)}{\sigma_m^2}$$

the **beta factor** of the $i$-th security.

It will turn out that the beta factor is directly related to the systematic risk of a security. We discuss this later on. First we state the famous CAPM formula.

**Theorem 5.3 (CAPM)**
*Suppose that the risk-free return R is lower than the expected return of the*

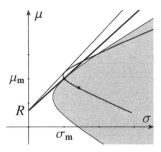

**Figure 5.1** Lack of tangency for portfolios built out of a security and the market portfolio, leads to portfolios with higher slope than that of the market portfolio.

*minimal variance portfolio (so that the market portfolio* **m** *exists). Then, for each i ≤ n, the expected return $\mu_i$ of the i-th asset in the portfolio is given by the formula*

$$\mu_i = R + \beta_i(\mu_m - R). \tag{5.1}$$

*Proof* As we know, the capital market line is tangent to the minimum variance line at the market portfolio point $(\sigma_m, \mu_m)$ (see Figure 4.8). Consider all portfolios built by means of the market portfolio and the *i*-th security. They form a hyperbola which we claim to be tangent to the capital market line at $(\sigma_m, \mu_m)$. Suppose that, on the contrary, this hyperbola intersects the CML. This clearly contradicts the fact that the slope of CML is maximal, see Figure 5.1

We compute the slope of the tangent line to the hyperbola at $(\sigma_m, \mu_m)$ and then we will use the fact that the slope of CML is the same. Denote the proportion of wealth invested in security *i* by *x* and that invested in the market portfolio by $1 - x$. We use **x** to denote the portfolio $\mathbf{x} = (x, 1 - x)$. The risk and return are of the form

$$\mu_x = x\mu_i + (1 - x)\mu_m,$$

$$\sigma_x = \sqrt{x^2\sigma_i^2 + (1 - x)^2\sigma_m^2 + 2x(1 - x)\mathrm{Cov}(K_i, K_m)},$$

and we compute their derivatives with respect to *x* at $x = 0$ to obtain

$$\left.\frac{\partial\mu_x}{\partial x}\right|_{x=0} = \mu_i - \mu_m,$$

$$\left.\frac{\partial\sigma_x}{\partial x}\right|_{x=0} = \frac{\mathrm{Cov}(K_i, K_m) - \sigma_m^2}{\sigma_m}.$$

The slope of the tangent is the ratio of these derivatives and we equate it to the slope of CML:

$$\frac{\mu_i - \mu_{\mathrm{m}}}{\frac{\mathrm{Cov}(K_i,K_{\mathrm{m}})-\sigma_{\mathrm{m}}^2}{\sigma_{\mathrm{m}}}} = \frac{\mu_{\mathrm{m}} - R}{\sigma_{\mathrm{m}}}.$$

Solving for $\mu_i$ we get

$$\mu_i = R + \frac{\mathrm{Cov}(K_i, K_{\mathrm{m}})}{\sigma_{\mathrm{m}}^2}(\mu_{\mathrm{m}} - R) = R + \beta_i(\mu_{\mathrm{m}} - R),$$

as required.                                                                              $\square$

The term $\beta_i(\mu_{\mathrm{m}} - R)$ in the CAPM formula (5.1) is called the **risk premium**. It represents the additional return required by an investor who faces the risk represented by the link of the portfolio to the whole market.

We see that the beta factor determines the expected return on a security. This means that beta quantifies the undiversifiable risk.

For a portfolio **w** we define

$$\beta_{\mathrm{w}} = \frac{\mathrm{Cov}(K_{\mathrm{w}}, K_{\mathrm{m}})}{\sigma_{\mathrm{m}}^2}.$$

Observe that for the market portfolio

$$\beta_{\mathrm{m}} = 1.$$

---

**Exercise 5.1**    Derive the CAPM formula

$$\mu_{\mathrm{w}} = R + \beta_{\mathrm{w}}(\mu_{\mathrm{m}} - R),$$

for a portfolio from the CAPM formula (5.1) for a single security.

---

**Exercise 5.2**    Assume that we can invest risk-free at a rate of return $R_1$ and borrow at $R_2$. Let $\mathbf{m}_1$ and $\mathbf{m}_2$ be the weights of the two tangency portfolios, corresponding to $R_1$ and $R_2$, respectively. Prove that

$$\mu_i = R_1 + \frac{\mathrm{Cov}(K_i, K_{\mathrm{m}_1})}{\sigma_{\mathrm{m}_1}^2}(\mu_{\mathrm{m}_1} - R_1),$$

$$\mu_i = R_2 + \frac{\mathrm{Cov}(K_i, K_{\mathrm{m}_2})}{\sigma_{\mathrm{m}_2}^2}(\mu_{\mathrm{m}_2} - R_2).$$

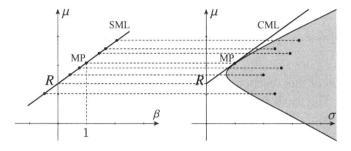

**Figure 5.2** Security market line (SML) and the capital market line (CML). MP is the market portfolio.

## 5.2 Security market line

We start by presenting an alternative proof of Theorem 5.3. We do this in a slightly more general context, formulating the result for a portfolio instead of a single security.

**Theorem 5.4**
*Suppose that the risk-free return $R$ is lower than the expected return of the minimal variance portfolio (so that the market portfolio $\mathbf{m}$ exists). Then, for any portfolio $\mathbf{w}$*

$$\mu_{\mathbf{w}} = R + \beta_{\mathbf{w}}(\mu_{\mathbf{m}} - R). \tag{5.2}$$

*Proof* From Theorem 4.10 we know that

$$\mathbf{m} = \frac{1}{\gamma} C^{-1}(\mu - R\mathbf{1}),$$

for $\gamma = \mathbf{1}^{\mathrm{T}} C^{-1}(\mu - R\mathbf{1})$. Applying Proposition 4.2,

$$\beta_{\mathbf{w}} = \frac{\mathrm{Cov}(K_{\mathbf{w}}, K_{\mathbf{m}})}{\sigma_{\mathbf{m}}^2} = \frac{\mathbf{w}^{\mathrm{T}} C\mathbf{m}}{\mathbf{m}^{\mathrm{T}} C\mathbf{m}} = \frac{\frac{1}{\gamma}\mathbf{w}^{\mathrm{T}}(\mu - R\mathbf{1})}{\frac{1}{\gamma}\mathbf{m}^{\mathrm{T}}(\mu - R\mathbf{1})}.$$

Since $\mathbf{w}^{\mathrm{T}}\mu = \mu_{\mathbf{w}}$, $\mathbf{m}^{\mathrm{T}}\mu = \mu_{\mathbf{m}}$ and $\mathbf{w}^{\mathrm{T}}\mathbf{1} = \mathbf{m}^{\mathrm{T}}\mathbf{1} = 1$, this gives

$$\beta_{\mathbf{w}} = \frac{\mu_{\mathbf{w}} - R}{\mu_{\mathbf{m}} - R}.$$

Rearranging we obtain (5.2). $\qquad\qquad\qquad\qquad\qquad\qquad\qquad\qquad\square$

The above proof is shorter than our first proof of Theorem 5.3. The first proof, however, is more intuitive, showing that the beta factor arises from purely geometric considerations.

From Theorem 5.4 we see that in the $(\beta, \mu)$-plane all portfolios lie on the straight line

$$\mu = R + \beta(\mu_m - R).$$

The graph of this function in the $(\beta, \mu)$-plane is called the **security market line**. This is shown in Figure 5.2 where the CML is also plotted for comparison.

In Figure 5.2, we see that we can have securities that remain attractive to investors despite having small expected returns and large variances, The reason for this is that these securities have negative betas, which implies that the covariance of the return on such an asset with the market is negative, meaning that the prices of such securities tend to move in the opposite direction to the market. Such assets are useful for hedging against negative trends on the market. A standard example of an asset with negative beta is gold, which can act as an insurance in a financial crisis.

The CAPM formula can be used to make investment decisions. Let us refer to the return from the CAPM formula as the **required return**. We can think of the required return as how the market perceives the expected return on a given security. Each individual investor, however, has his own beliefs. If for a given security an investor thinks, due to some additional information he has, that the true expected return is higher than the required return,

$$\mu_i > R + \beta_i(\mu_m - R),$$

then this means that the security is underpriced. He should then invest in the security. If more investors share this belief, they will do the same, and as a result of the demand created the price goes up, which pushes the expected return down. On the other hand, if

$$\mu_i < R + \beta_i(\mu_m - R),$$

investors want to sell or even short-sell the security, the price falls because of the excess supply, and the expected return increases. In both cases we should therefore observe price adjustments restoring the CAPM formula to an equilibrium.

Apart from illustrating the market equilibrium, CAPM has applications in analysing the performance of various investments. The right-hand side of CAPM gives the target return and this is compared with the realised return. The difference: the realised return minus the target return, is called the **Jensen index**. A possible goal is to achieve a positive value of this index, the higher the better.

Another approach to the evaluation of performance comes from comparing a portfolio's market price of risk with an agreed benchmark. For a given portfolio **w** the market price of risk is defined as the excess return per unit risk:

$$MPR_{\mathbf{w}} = \frac{\mu_{\mathbf{w}} - R}{\sigma_{\mathbf{w}}}.$$

This quantity is referred to as the Sharpe index or **Sharpe ratio**. The benchmark is the market price of risk for the market portfolio, in other words the slope of the CML:

$$MPR_{\mathbf{m}} = \frac{\mu_{\mathbf{m}} - R}{\sigma_{\mathbf{m}}}.$$

The investor will clearly seek to maximise the Sharpe index of his portfolio.

## 5.3  Characteristic line

The CAPM formula is concerned with expectations. Our next step is to consider the returns themselves, that is the random variables

$$K_{\mathbf{w}} = R + \beta_{\mathbf{w}}(K_{\mathbf{m}} - R) + e_{\mathbf{w}}, \tag{5.3}$$

where the error $e_{\mathbf{w}}$ is a random variable defined as

$$e_{\mathbf{w}} = K_{\mathbf{w}} - [R + \beta_{\mathbf{w}}(K_{\mathbf{m}} - R)].$$

From the CAPM formula (5.2) we have

$$\mathbb{E}(e_{\mathbf{w}}) = \mu_{\mathbf{w}} - [R + \beta_{\mathbf{w}}(\mu_{\mathbf{m}} - R)] = 0.$$

It is interesting to observe that the principle of error minimisation implies the form of the beta coefficient:

**Proposition 5.5**
*Given a portfolio* **w**, *let* $e_{\mathbf{w}} = K_{\mathbf{w}} - R - \beta(K_{\mathbf{m}} - R)$ *for some number* $\beta$. *The variance of* $e_{\mathbf{w}}$ *is minimal for* $\beta = \frac{\mathrm{Cov}(K_{\mathbf{w}}, K_{\mathbf{m}})}{\mathrm{Var}(K_{\mathbf{m}})}$.

*Proof*   We can compute the variance of $e_{\mathbf{w}}$ as

$$
\begin{aligned}
\mathrm{Var}(e_{\mathbf{w}}) &= \mathrm{Var}(K_{\mathbf{w}} - R - \beta(K_{\mathbf{m}} - R)) \\
&= \mathrm{Var}(K_{\mathbf{w}} - \beta K_{\mathbf{m}}) \qquad (\mathrm{Var}(X + a) = \mathrm{Var}(X) \text{ for constant } a) \\
&= \mathrm{Var}(K_{\mathbf{w}}) + \mathrm{Var}(-\beta K_{\mathbf{m}}) + 2\mathrm{Cov}(K_{\mathbf{w}}, -\beta K_{\mathbf{m}}) \\
&= \mathrm{Var}(K_{\mathbf{w}}) + \beta^2 \mathrm{Var}(K_{\mathbf{m}}) - 2\beta \mathrm{Cov}(K_{\mathbf{w}}, K_{\mathbf{m}}).
\end{aligned}
$$

This is a quadratic function of $\beta$ with a positive coefficient for $\beta^2$. The minimum is found when

$$0 = 2\beta \text{Var}(K_{\mathbf{m}}) - 2\text{Cov}(K_{\mathbf{w}}, K_{\mathbf{m}}),$$

hence

$$\beta = \frac{\text{Cov}(K_{\mathbf{w}}, K_{\mathbf{m}})}{\text{Var}(K_{\mathbf{m}})},$$

which concludes the proof. □

The relation between the returns (5.3) and the connection to the minimising of the variance of the error provides a method of finding the beta from historical data. Plotting the realised past returns on the securities against the realised returns on the market portfolio enables one to find the **line of best fit**, also known as the **security characteristic line**. For an asset with return $K_i$ we have

$$K_i - R = \alpha_i + \beta_i (K_{\mathbf{m}} - R) + e_i$$

where $e_i$ is the error, with $\mathbb{E}(e_i) = 0$, and $\alpha_i$ is called the alpha, or **abnormal return** of the asset. By CAPM theory, the coefficient $\alpha_i$ should be zero. In practice though, markets do not strictly follow the theory and non-zero abnormal returns can be observed from historical data.

If $\hat{K}_i^1, \ldots, \hat{K}_i^d$ and $\hat{K}_{\mathbf{m}}^1, \ldots, \hat{K}_{\mathbf{m}}^d$ are the historical realised returns, then we can find the parameters of the characteristic line using the least square method. It will be convenient to use the notation

$$\begin{aligned} x_j &= \hat{K}_{\mathbf{m}}^j - R, \\ y_j &= \hat{K}_i^j - R, \end{aligned} \quad \text{for } j = 1, \ldots, d,$$

to stand for historical excess returns. We define a function

$$f(\alpha, \beta) = \sum_{j=1}^{d} \left( \hat{K}_i^j - R - \alpha - \beta \left( \hat{K}_{\mathbf{m}}^j - R \right) \right)^2 = \sum_{j=1}^{d} \left( y_j - \alpha - \beta x_j \right)^2,$$

and find its minimum by solving the system of equations

$$\begin{aligned} \frac{\partial f}{\partial \alpha} &= 0, \\ \frac{\partial f}{\partial \beta} &= 0. \end{aligned} \tag{5.4}$$

This leads to

$$\begin{aligned} \beta &= \frac{\overline{xy} - \overline{x}\,\overline{y}}{\overline{xx} - \overline{x}\,\overline{x}}, \\ \alpha &= \bar{y} - \beta \bar{x}, \end{aligned} \tag{5.5}$$

where

$$\bar{x} = \frac{1}{d} \sum_{j=1}^{d} x_j, \qquad \overline{xy} = \frac{1}{d} \sum_{j=1}^{d} x_j y_j,$$
$$\bar{y} = \frac{1}{d} \sum_{j=1}^{d} y_j, \qquad \overline{xx} = \frac{1}{d} \sum_{j=1}^{d} x_j^2.$$

Formula (5.5) can be used to estimate the beta factor of a security, based on historical data.

---

**Exercise 5.3**  Derive (5.5) from (5.4).

---

We conclude this chapter by returning to (5.3), in order to compute the variance of $K_w$. This will highlight from yet another angle the fact that the beta factor quantifies the undiversifiable risk.

**Proposition 5.6**
*The variance of the return on a portfolio can be expressed as*

$$\sigma_w^2 = \beta_w^2 \sigma_m^2 + \text{Var}(e_w). \tag{5.6}$$

*Proof*  First we find the covariance between $e_w$ and $K_m$

$$\begin{aligned}
\text{Cov}(K_m, e_w) &= \text{Cov}(K_m, K_w - R - \beta_w(K_m - R)) \\
&= \text{Cov}(K_m, K_w) - \beta_w \text{Cov}(K_m, K_m) \\
&= 0.
\end{aligned}$$

Next

$$\begin{aligned}
\text{Var}(K_w) &= \text{Var}(R + \beta_w(K_m - R) + e_w) \\
&= \text{Var}(\beta_w K_m + e_w) \qquad \text{(since } \text{Var}(X + a) = \text{Var}(X)) \\
&= \beta_w^2 \text{Var}(K_m) + \text{Var}(e_w) + 2\beta_w \text{Cov}(K_m, e_w) \\
&= \beta_w^2 \text{Var}(K_m) + \text{Var}(e_w),
\end{aligned}$$

which concludes the proof.  $\square$

The formula (5.6) sheds more light on the distinction between the two kinds of risk. The first term represents the systematic risk that cannot be avoided by adding more securities to the portfolio and it is measured by the beta coefficient. The second term is the diversifiable part of the risk. Taking $\mathbf{w} = \mathbf{m}$, since $\beta_m = 1$,

$$e_m = K_m - R - \beta_m(K_m - R) = 0,$$

hence the term $\text{Var}(e_w)$ can be discarded if we invest in the market portfolio or in a portfolio sufficiently diversified to serve in practice as its substitute.

# 6

---

# Utility functions

---

Making the fundamental assumption that rational investors prefer more wealth to less, we impose preference relations on the set of possible final (time 1) positions of an investor who, at time 0, invests a fixed sum in a range of risky securities. In this chapter we simplify the analysis by restricting to a finite sample space, so that there are $N$ possible outcomes. We state axioms for preference relations among the $N$-dimensional vectors representing the possible outcomes for his final wealth. Each such relation is expressed in terms of a real-valued function called a utility.

We focus on utilities arising as expectations, and show that utility maximisation is closely related to the No Arbitrage Principle (NAP), which is discussed in detail in [DMFM]. This leads to the introduction of state prices (equivalently, risk-neutral probabilities). We solve the utility maximisation problem in terms of minimising expectations with respect to the set of possible state price vectors. We also explore the relationship between quadratic utility functions and the CAPM and conclude with a brief study of risk aversion measures.

## 6.1   Basic notions and axioms

We begin with recalling some basic probability notation. In this chapter we restrict our attention to the case of a discrete probability space, $\Omega =$

$\{\omega_1, \ldots, \omega_N\}$, with

$$P(\{\omega_i\}) = p_i > 0.$$

The prices of securities are denoted by $S_j(0)$, the initial prices, and

$$S_j(1, \omega_i) = S_j(1)(\omega_i),$$

the prices at the end of the period, which depend on the state. Portfolios will be described by the numbers $x_j$ of securities held. A portfolio is represented by a vector $\mathbf{x} = (x_1, \ldots, x_n)$. We denote the initial wealth of the investor by $V$, so the formation of a portfolio is subject to the bound

$$\sum_{j=1}^{n} x_j S_j(0) = V.$$

The final wealth is a random variable determined by the portfolio chosen, and we denote it by $V_{\mathbf{x}}(1)$. In the state $\omega_i$ it takes the value

$$V_{\mathbf{x}}(1, \omega_i) = \sum_{j=1}^{n} x_j S_j(1, \omega_i).$$

We will find it convenient to use the following matrix notation:

$$\mathbf{S}(0) = \begin{bmatrix} S_1(0) & \cdots & S_n(0) \end{bmatrix}, \qquad \mathbf{S}(1) = \begin{bmatrix} s_{11} & \cdots & s_{1n} \\ \vdots & & \vdots \\ s_{N1} & \cdots & s_{Nn} \end{bmatrix}, \qquad (6.1)$$

where

$$s_{ij} = S_j(1, \omega_i).$$

We can then write

$$V_{\mathbf{x}}(0) = \mathbf{S}(0)\mathbf{x},$$
$$V_{\mathbf{x}}(1) = \mathbf{S}(1)\mathbf{x}. \qquad (6.2)$$

The matrix $\mathbf{S}(1)$ represents a linear map, which we assume to be one-to-one. This means in particular that the number of rows ($N$) is not less than the number of columns ($n$) and that the matrix has maximal rank, namely $n$. In other words, the number $N$ of scenarios (members of $\Omega$) is at least as great as the number of assets ($n$).

At times we will find it convenient to identify a random variable $X : \Omega \to \mathbb{R}$ with a vector $X = (X_1, \ldots, X_N) \in \mathbb{R}^N$, by which we mean that

$$X_i = X(\omega_i).$$

The amount $V_x(1)$ can be consumed by the investor. This motivates the name **feasible consumption set** for the set

$$FCS = \left\{ X \in \mathbb{R}^N \mid X_i \geq 0, \ X = V_x(1) \text{ where } V_x(0) = V \right\}.$$

We assume that the investor can decide between any two possible final consumptions from the $FCS$. So we assume that a binary relation on $FCS$ is given: for $X, Y \in FCS$ we write $X \preceq Y$ to mean that the investor prefers $Y$ to $X$.

**Axiom 1 (transitivity)** If $X \preceq Y$ and $Y \preceq Z$ then $X \preceq Z$.

This axiom is sometimes called the consistency axiom since it excludes irrational preferences.

**Axiom 2 (completeness)** For all $X, Y$ either $X \preceq Y$ or $Y \preceq X$.

Thus we assume that each individual can always decide which of two given positions he prefers.

If Axioms 1 and 2 are satisfied, we call $\preceq$ a **preference relation**. In practice, a preference relation may be difficult to specify. An alternative approach is based on employing a so-called utility.

**Definition 6.1**
A function $U : \mathbb{R}^N \to \mathbb{R}$ is called a **utility** if it is strictly increasing with respect to each variable, differentiable and strictly concave.

Using a utility $U$ we can define the relation

$$X \preceq_U Y \quad \text{if and only if } U(X) \leq U(Y).$$

---

**Exercise 6.1**   Show that when $U$ is a utility, $\preceq_U$ is a preference relation.

---

Not every preference relation can be represented by a utility. We give an example of this in the form of an exercise.

---

**Exercise 6.2**   The lexicographic order $\preceq_{\text{lex}}$ on $\mathbb{R}^2$ is defined as follows: for $\mathbf{p} = (p_1, p_2)$ and $\mathbf{q} = (q_1, q_2)$

$$\mathbf{p} \preceq_{\text{lex}} \mathbf{q}$$

if and only if

$$p_1 < q_1 \quad \text{or} \quad p_1 = q_1 \text{ and } p_2 \le q_2.$$

Show that $\le_{\text{lex}}$ is a preference relation that cannot be represented by a utility.

A particular case of utility is the expected utility, determined by means of a utility function.

**Definition 6.2**
We say that $u : \mathbb{R} \to \mathbb{R}$ is a **utility function** if it is strictly increasing, differentiable and strictly concave.

**Proposition 6.3**
*If $u : \mathbb{R} \to \mathbb{R}$ is a utility function, then $U$ defined by*

$$U(X) = \mathbb{E}(u(X))$$

*is a utility.*

*Proof* The function $U$ can be written as

$$U(X) = \mathbb{E}(u(X)) = \sum_{i=1}^{N} p_i u(X_i).$$

We need to show that $U$ is strictly increasing with respect to each variable, differentiable and strictly concave.

The function $U$ is differentiable since $u$ is differentiable; in particular

$$U'(X) = \left[ \begin{array}{cccc} \frac{\partial U}{\partial X_1}(X) & \frac{\partial U}{\partial X_2}(X) & \cdots & \frac{\partial U}{\partial X_N}(X) \end{array} \right]$$
$$= \left[ \begin{array}{cccc} p_1 u'(X_1) & p_2 u'(X_2) & \cdots & p_N u'(X_N) \end{array} \right].$$

The function $u$ is strictly increasing, hence $u'(x) > 0$ for all $x \in \mathbb{R}$. We also have $p_i > 0$ for $i = 1, \ldots, N$, hence

$$\frac{\partial U}{\partial X_i}(X) = p_i u'(X_i) > 0.$$

This means that $U$ is strictly increasing with respect to each variable.

Since $u$ is strictly concave, for any $x_1 \ne x_2$ and any $\lambda \in (0, 1)$

$$u(\lambda x_1 + (1 - \lambda)x_2) > \lambda u(x_1) + (1 - \lambda)u(x_2).$$

For any $X, Y \in \mathbb{R}^N$ this gives

$$U(\lambda X + (1 - \lambda) Y) = U(\lambda X_1 + (1 - \lambda) Y_1, \ldots, \lambda X_N + (1 - \lambda) Y_N)$$

$$= \sum_{i=1}^{N} p_i u(\lambda X_i + (1 - \lambda) Y_i)$$

$$> \sum_{i=1}^{N} p_i [\lambda u(X_i) + (1 - \lambda) u(Y_i)]$$

$$= \lambda U(X) + (1 - \lambda) U(Y),$$

which means that $U$ is strictly concave.                    □

**Definition 6.4**

We say that a utility $U$ is a **von Neumann–Morgenstern utility** if there exists a utility function $u$ such that

$$U(X) = \mathbb{E}(u(X)).$$

The crucial feature of a von Neumann–Morgenstern utility is that it is determined by a single-variable function $u$.

**Example 6.5**

Typical examples of utility functions are as follows:

(i) Exponential: $u(x) = -e^{-ax}$;

(ii) Logarithmic: $u(x) = \ln x$;

(iii) Power: $u(x) = ax^a$ for $a \leq 1$;

(iv) Quadratic: $u(x) = x - \frac{1}{2}bx^2$ (which is increasing only for $x < \frac{1}{b}$).

---

**Exercise 6.3**  Verify that the functions from Example 6.5 satisfy the conditions of Definition 6.2.

---

## 6.2  Utility maximisation

An investor wishes to maximise his utility, meaning that he seeks a solution to the problem

$$\max\{U(X) : X \in FCS\}. \tag{6.3}$$

The existence of a solution to this problem is related to the notion of arbitrage.

**Definition 6.6**
We say that a portfolio $\mathbf{x} = (x_1, \ldots, x_n)$ is an **arbitrage opportunity** if $V_{\mathbf{x}}(0) = 0$ and $V_{\mathbf{x}}(1) \geq 0$ with $V_{\mathbf{x}}(1, \omega_i) > 0$ for at least one $\omega_i \in \Omega$.

A fundamental assumption of mathematical finance is that arbitrage opportunities do not exist (this is known as the No Arbitrage Principle; see [DMFM] and [BSM] for extensive discussions). The next result explains how this principle relates to utility maximisation.

**Theorem 6.7**
*If there is a solution to problem (6.3), then there is no arbitrage. Conversely, if U is continuous and there is no arbitrage, then problem (6.3) has a solution.*

*Proof* Suppose there is an $\mathbf{x}^* \in \mathbb{R}^n$ such that $V_{\mathbf{x}^*}(1) \in FCS$ is a solution of (6.3), meaning that

$$U(X) \leq U(V_{\mathbf{x}^*}(1)), \qquad (6.4)$$

for any feasible consumption $X$. Suppose that there exists an arbitrage opportunity $\mathbf{y}$. Take $\mathbf{z} = \mathbf{x}^* + \mathbf{y}$. Since $V_{\mathbf{y}}(0) = 0$, and $V_{\mathbf{y}}(1, \omega_i) \geq 0$ for any $\omega_i \in \Omega$,

$$V_{\mathbf{z}}(0) = V_{\mathbf{y}}(0) + V_{\mathbf{x}^*}(0) = V_{\mathbf{x}^*}(0) = V,$$
$$V_{\mathbf{z}}(1, \omega_i) = V_{\mathbf{y}}(1, \omega_i) + V_{\mathbf{x}^*}(1, \omega_i) \geq V_{\mathbf{x}^*}(1, \omega_i) \geq 0,$$

so $\mathbf{z}$ is feasible. We know that $V_{\mathbf{y}}(1, \omega_k) > 0$ for some $\omega_k \in \Omega$, which implies that

$$V_{\mathbf{z}}(1, \omega_k) > V_{\mathbf{x}^*}(1, \omega_k).$$

This means that since $U$ is strictly increasing in each variable,

$$U(V_{\mathbf{z}}(1)) > U(V_{\mathbf{x}}(1)),$$

which contradicts (6.4). We have thus proved that there is no arbitrage.

We now show that no arbitrage implies existence of a solution of (6.3). We shall use the fact that a continuous function on a closed bounded subset of $\mathbb{R}^N$ admits a maximum.

The set $FCS$, which is a subset of $\mathbb{R}^N$, is closed, since $U$ is continuous and defines $FCS$ by weak inequalities. So to obtain an maximum it is sufficient to show that $FCS$ is bounded. Suppose that, on the contrary, there is a sequence $\mathbf{x}_k$ such that $\left\|V_{\mathbf{x}_k}(1)\right\| \to \infty$ as $k \to \infty$. (Here $\|Z\| = \max_{i \le N} |z_i|$ for any $Z = (z_1, \ldots, z_N)$ in $\mathbb{R}^N$.) Let

$$C = \max_{\substack{j=1,\ldots,n \\ i=1,\ldots,N}} \left|S_j(1, \omega_i)\right|.$$

Observing that for any $\mathbf{y} = (y_1, \ldots, y_n)$ and any $i \le N$,

$$\left|V_{\mathbf{y}}(1, \omega_i)\right| = \left|\sum_{j=1}^{n} y_j S_j(1, \omega_i)\right| \le C \max_{j=1,\ldots,n} |y_j|.$$

This shows that we can only have $\left\|V_{\mathbf{x}_k}(1)\right\| \to \infty$ when $\|\mathbf{x}_k\| \to \infty$. The sequence $\mathbf{z}_k = \frac{\mathbf{x}_k}{\|\mathbf{x}_k\|}$ is bounded, hence has a subsequence convergent to a limit $\mathbf{z}$. We show that $\mathbf{z}$ is an arbitrage opportunity, which provides the contradiction we seek. First,

$$V_{\mathbf{z}_k}(0) = \sum_{j=1}^{n} (\mathbf{z}_k)_j \, S_j(0) = \frac{1}{\|\mathbf{x}_k\|} \sum_{j=1}^{n} (\mathbf{x}_k)_j S_j(0) = \frac{V}{\|\mathbf{x}_k\|} \to 0,$$

so $V_{\mathbf{z}}(0) = 0$. Second, for any $\omega_i \in \Omega$

$$V_{\mathbf{z}_k}(1, \omega_i) = \frac{1}{\|\mathbf{x}_k\|} \sum_{j=1}^{n} (\mathbf{x}_k)_j S_j(1, \omega_i) = \frac{1}{\|\mathbf{x}_k\|} V_{\mathbf{x}_k}(1, \omega_i) \ge 0,$$

by the definition of $FCS$, and this inequality is preserved in the limit, giving

$$V_{\mathbf{z}}(1, \omega_i) \ge 0. \tag{6.5}$$

Since $\mathbf{S}(1)$ is one-to-one, if we had $\mathbf{S}(1)\mathbf{z} = 0$, then $\mathbf{z}$ would need to be equal to zero. This is not possible since $\|\mathbf{z}\| = 1$, hence

$$V_{\mathbf{z}}(1) = \mathbf{S}(1)\mathbf{z} \ne 0.$$

Combined with (6.5), this means that $V_{\mathbf{z}}(1, \omega_i) > 0$ for some $\omega_i \in \Omega$, showing that $\mathbf{z}$ is an arbitrage opportunity.                                  $\square$

We now turn to the question of the relation between the security prices at time 0 and 1.

**Definition 6.8**
We say that $\boldsymbol{\pi} = (\pi_1, \ldots, \pi_N)$ is a vector of **state prices**, if $\pi_i > 0$ for $i = 1, \ldots, N$, and

$$S_j(0) = \sum_{i=1}^{N} \pi_i S_j(1, \omega_i). \tag{6.6}$$

Condition (6.6) can be written in matrix notation as

$$\mathbf{S}(0) = \boldsymbol{\pi}^{\mathrm{T}} \mathbf{S}(1).$$ (6.7)

We have the following relation linking the value of a strategy with state prices.

**Lemma 6.9**
*For any* $\mathbf{x} \in \mathbb{R}^n$

$$V_{\mathbf{x}}(0) = \sum_{i=1}^{N} \pi_i V_{\mathbf{x}}(1, \omega_i).$$

*Proof*  The claim follows from computing

$$V_{\mathbf{x}}(0) = \sum_{j=1}^{n} x_j S_j(0)$$

$$= \sum_{j=1}^{n} x_j \sum_{i=1}^{N} \pi_i S_j(1, \omega_i) \qquad \text{(from (6.6))}$$

$$= \sum_{i=1}^{N} \pi_i \sum_{j=1}^{n} x_j S_j(1, \omega_i)$$

$$= \sum_{i=1}^{N} \pi_i V_{\mathbf{x}}(1, \omega_i).$$

$$\square$$

Suppose that one of the securities is risk-free, that is, $S_1(1, \omega_i) = 1$ for all $i$, say. Then

$$S_1(0) = \sum_{i=1}^{N} \pi_i,$$

which is the price of a sure unit of currency (say euro) to be received at time 1, that is, it is the discount factor. We then have the relation with the risk-free return

$$\sum_{i=1}^{N} \pi_i = \frac{1}{1+R}.$$ (6.8)

State prices are related to risk-neutral probabilities.

**Definition 6.10**
We say that a probability $Q$

$$Q(\{\omega_i\}) = q_i \qquad \text{for } i = 1, \ldots, N,$$

is a **risk-neutral probability** if for any $j \in \{1, \ldots, n\}$

$$S_j(0) = \frac{1}{1+R} \mathbb{E}_Q(S_j(1)) = \frac{1}{1+R} \sum_{i=1}^{N} q_i S_j(1, \omega_i). \tag{6.9}$$

One of the fundamental results in mathematical finance, referred to in the literature as the first fundamental theorem of asset pricing, states that lack of arbitrage is equivalent to the existence of a risk-neutral probability. (For details the reader is directed to [DMFM].) Comparing (6.6) with (6.9), we see that

$$\pi_i = \frac{q_i}{1+R},$$

thus existence of state prices is equivalent to the No Arbitrage Principle. However, the No Arbitrage Principle does not guarantee that a risk-neutral probability is unique. For this we need the notion of completeness of the market model.

**Definition 6.11**
A market model is **complete** if for any $H : \Omega \to \mathbb{R}$, there exists an $\mathbf{x} \in \mathbb{R}^n$ such that

$$V_{\mathbf{x}}(1) = H.$$

When the market model is arbitrage-free and complete, the risk-neutral probability exists and is unique. This result is referred to as the second fundamental theorem of asset pricing. Details and a proof can be found in [DMFM]. Existence and uniqueness of the risk-neutral probability is therefore equivalent to existence and uniqueness of state prices.

We now show how state prices are related to the optimal solution of the utility maximisation problem.

**Theorem 6.12**
*Assume that $X^*$ is a strictly positive solution (meaning that $X^*(\omega_i) > 0$ for all $\omega_i \in \Omega$) of the maximisation problem (6.3). Then there is a number $\lambda$ such that*

$$\pi_i = \lambda \frac{\partial U}{\partial X_i}(X^*) \tag{6.10}$$

*are state prices.*

*Proof*  Let us consider two functions $f, g : \mathbb{R}^n \to \mathbb{R}$, defined by

$$f(\mathbf{x}) = U(V_{\mathbf{x}}(1)),$$
$$g(\mathbf{x}) = V_{\mathbf{x}}(0) - V.$$

The problem (6.3) is equivalent to solving

$$\max f(\mathbf{x}),$$
$$\text{subject to: } g(\mathbf{x}) = 0.$$

Let $\mathbf{x}^*$ be the solution of the problem, implying that $X^* = V_{\mathbf{x}^*}(1)$. By the method of Lagrange multipliers, there exists an $\alpha \in \mathbb{R}$ such that

$$\nabla f(\mathbf{x}^*) - \alpha \nabla g(\mathbf{x}^*) = 0. \tag{6.11}$$

The $j$-th coordinate of $\nabla g$ is equal to

$$\frac{\partial g}{\partial x_j} = \frac{\partial}{\partial x_j} \sum_{k=1}^{n} x_k S_k(0) = S_j(0).$$

Let $(V_{\mathbf{x}}(1))_i$ denote the $i$-th coordinate of the $N$-dimensional vector $V_{\mathbf{x}}(1)$. Using the chain rule we obtain

$$\frac{\partial f}{\partial x_j}(\mathbf{x}) = \frac{\partial}{\partial x_j} U(V_{\mathbf{x}}(1))$$

$$= \sum_{i=1}^{N} \frac{\partial U}{\partial X_i}(V_{\mathbf{x}}(1)) \frac{\partial}{\partial x_j}(V_{\mathbf{x}}(1))_i$$

$$= \sum_{i=1}^{N} \frac{\partial U}{\partial X_i}(V_{\mathbf{x}}(1)) \frac{\partial}{\partial x_j} \left( \sum_{k=1}^{n} x_k S_k(1, \omega_i) \right)$$

$$= \sum_{i=1}^{N} \frac{\partial U}{\partial X_i}(V_{\mathbf{x}}(1)) S_j(1, \omega_i),$$

hence, since $V_{\mathbf{x}^*}(1) = X^*$,

$$\frac{\partial f}{\partial x_j}(\mathbf{x}^*) = \sum_{i=1}^{N} \frac{\partial U}{\partial X_i}(X^*) S_j(1, \omega_i).$$

Taking $\lambda = \frac{1}{\alpha}$ and looking at the $j$-th coordinate of (6.11) gives

$$S_j(0) = \sum_{i=1}^{N} \lambda \frac{\partial U}{\partial X_i}(X^*) S_j(1, \omega_i).$$

Comparing with (6.6) we see that for each $i \leq N$,

$$\pi_i = \lambda \frac{\partial U}{\partial X_i}(X^*),$$

satisfies the condition required to be a state price. $\qquad\square$

**Corollary 6.13**
*For the particular case of expected utility, where $U(X) = \mathbb{E}(u(X))$, the state prices take the form*

$$\pi_i = \lambda u'(X^*(\omega_i))p_i.$$

*Proof*   Since we are dealing with expected utility

$$U(X_1,\ldots,X_N) = \sum_{k=1}^{N} p_k u(X_k),$$

so

$$\frac{\partial U}{\partial X_i}(X_1,\ldots,X_N) = u'(X_i)\,p_i,$$

hence

$$\frac{\partial U}{\partial X_i}(X^*) = u'(X^*(\omega_i))p_i,$$

and combined with (6.10) this implies the claim.                    □

Theorem 6.12 can be used to find the solution of the optimisation problem. We focus on the particular case of expected utility $U(X) = \mathbb{E}(u(X))$.

**Theorem 6.14**
*Assume that $U(X) = \mathbb{E}(u(X))$. If $X^* = (X_1^*,\ldots,X_N^*)$ is a solution of the problem (6.3), then, with $(u')^{-1}$ denoting the inverse function of $u'$, we obtain*

$$X_i^* = (u')^{-1}\left(\frac{\pi_i}{\lambda p_i}\right), \qquad (6.12)$$

*where $\lambda$ is determined by the condition*

$$V = \sum_{i=1}^{N} \pi_i (u')^{-1}\left(\frac{\pi_i}{\lambda p_i}\right). \qquad (6.13)$$

*Proof*   The assertion (6.12) follows directly from Corollary 6.13.
Since $X^* = V_{\mathbf{x}^*}(1)$, by Lemma 6.9

$$V = V_{\mathbf{x}^*}(0) = \sum_{i=1}^{N} \pi_i V_{\mathbf{x}^*}(1,\omega_i) = \sum_{i=1}^{N} \pi_i X^*(\omega_i).$$

Substituting (6.12) into the above equation gives (6.13).                    □

We observe that (6.12) and (6.13) combined, constitute of $N+1$ equations with $N+1$ unknowns. Thus Theorem 6.14 provides a tool for finding candidates for the solution of the optimisation problem, by way of solving a system of equations. The system of equations provides a necessary condition for the solution of (6.3). Each solution depends on the choice of the state prices. In cases where the state prices are not uniquely determined, we can have solutions of (6.12)–(6.13) that are not solutions of the optimisation problem.

**Example 6.15**

In this example we consider the case of a logarithmic utility function $u(x) = \ln(x)$. Then $u'(x) = \frac{1}{x}$ and $(u')^{-1}(y) = \frac{1}{y}$. By (6.12) this gives

$$X^*(\omega_i) = (u')^{-1}\left(\frac{\pi_i}{\lambda p_i}\right) = \frac{\lambda p_i}{\pi_i}, \tag{6.14}$$

and this $\lambda$ is determined by (6.13) so that

$$V = \sum_{i=1}^{N} \pi_i (u')^{-1}\left(\frac{\pi_i}{\lambda p_i}\right) = \sum_{i=1}^{N} \pi_i \frac{\lambda p_i}{\pi_i} = \lambda. \tag{6.15}$$

We consider a trinomial model with a single risky security with today's price $S(0) = 100$ and future prices

$$S(1) = \begin{cases} S^u = S(0)(1+u) & \text{with probability } \frac{1}{4}, \\ S^m = S(0)(1+m) & \text{with probability } \frac{1}{2}, \\ S^d = S(0)(1+d) & \text{with probability } \frac{1}{4}, \end{cases}$$

with $u = 0.1$, $m = 0$ and $d = -0.1$. We consider $V = 100$ and for simplicity assume that we can invest risk-free at $R = 0$.

From (6.6) and (6.8), state prices satisfy

$$S(0) = \pi_1 S(0)(1+u) + \pi_2 S(0)(1+m) + \pi_3 S(0)(1+d),$$
$$1 = \pi_1 + \pi_2 + \pi_3.$$

This system of equations admits infinitely many solutions:

$$\pi_1(x) = x,$$
$$\pi_2(x) = \frac{x(d-u)-d}{m-d},$$
$$\pi_3(x) = \frac{x(u-m)+m}{m-d}.$$

For each solution we can use (6.14) to compute $X^*$. Below we see results

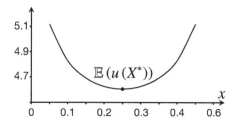

**Figure 6.1** Optimal expected utility from Example 6.15.

for a selection of choices of $x$:

| $x$ | $X^*(\omega_1)$ | $X^*(\omega_2)$ | $X^*(\omega_3)$ | $\mathbb{E}(u(X^*))$ |
|------|------|------|------|------|
| 0.1 | 250 | $\frac{250}{4}$ | 250 | 4.83 |
| 0.2 | 125 | $\frac{250}{3}$ | 125 | 4.63 |
| 0.25 | 100 | 100 | 100 | 4.6 |
| 0.3 | $\frac{250}{3}$ | 125 | $\frac{250}{3}$ | 4.63 |
| 0.4 | $\frac{250}{4}$ | 250 | $\frac{250}{4}$ | 4.83 |

It appears that, out of the above, the $X^*$ for $x = 0.1$ and $x = 0.4$ have the highest expected utility. But $X^*$ associated both with $x = 0.1$ and $x = 0.4$ is not attainable though by means of a portfolio. Only $X^*$ for $x = 0.25$ is attainable, by investing $V$ risk free.

We see therefore that not all solutions of (6.12)–(6.13) need to be solutions of the optimisation problem. In fact, only the solution with the smallest expected utility turns out to be feasible (see Figure 6.1).

---

**Exercise 6.4** Prove that $X^* = 100$ is the solution to the problem posed in Example 6.15.

---

In Example 6.15 the solution of the optimisation problem turned out to have the smallest utility amongst the solutions of (6.12)–(6.13). We now show that this should not be a surprise. First we introduce some notation and an auxiliary lemma.

For a fixed state price vector $\pi = (\pi_1, \ldots, \pi_N)$ we use the following notation:

$$\mathcal{X}(\pi) = \{X \in \mathbb{R}^N \mid X > 0, \pi^T X = V\}.$$

**Lemma 6.16**
*If $X_\pi^* = (X_{\pi,1}^*, \ldots X_{\pi,N}^*) \in \mathcal{X}(\pi)$ is a solution of*

$$\max\{\mathbb{E}(u(X)) : X \in \mathcal{X}(\pi)\}$$

*then there exists a $\lambda$ such that*

$$X_{\pi,i}^* = (u')^{-1}\left(\frac{\pi_i}{\lambda p_i}\right),$$

$$V = \sum_{i=1}^N \pi_i (u')^{-1}\left(\frac{\pi_i}{\lambda p_i}\right).$$

*Proof*  The claim follows from the method of Lagrange multipliers (Theorem 3.3), taking

$$f(X_1, \ldots, X_N) = \sum_{i=1}^N p_i u(X_i)$$

and

$$g(X_1, \ldots, X_N) = \sum_{i=1}^N \pi_i X_i - V,$$

and is left as an exercise.  □

---

**Exercise 6.5**   Prove Lemma 6.16.

---

**Theorem 6.17**
*Assume that $U(X) = \mathbb{E}(u(X))$. Let $\Pi$ denote the set of all state price vectors. If the model admits a strictly positive solution $X^*$ of the optimisation problem (6.3), then*

$$\mathbb{E}(u(X^*)) = \min_{\pi \in \Pi} \mathbb{E}(u(X_\pi^*)).$$

*Proof*  By Lemma 6.9, for any $\pi \in \Pi$

$$\pi^T X^* = \sum_{j=1}^n \pi_j X_j^* = V$$

shows that $X^* \in X(\pi)$, hence

$$\mathbb{E}(u(X^*)) \le \max_{X \in X(\pi)} \mathbb{E}(u(X)) = \mathbb{E}(u(X_\pi^*)),$$

and therefore

$$\mathbb{E}(u(X^*)) \le \min_{\pi \in \Pi} \mathbb{E}(u(X_\pi^*)).$$

To obtain the inequality in the opposite direction, let $v = (v_1, \dots, v_N)$ be the state price vector from Theorem 6.12, i.e.

$$v_i = \lambda \frac{\partial U}{\partial X_i}(X^*).$$

By Corollary 6.13 and Theorem 6.14

$$v_i = \lambda u'(X_i^*) p_i, \tag{6.16}$$

where $\lambda$ is chosen to satisfy

$$V = \sum_{i=1}^{N} v_i (u')^{-1} \left( \frac{v_i}{\lambda p_i} \right).$$

By Lemma 6.16 we know that

$$X_{v,i}^* = (u')^{-1} \left( \frac{v_i}{\lambda p_i} \right).$$

Substituting (6.16) into the above we see that $X_{v,i}^* = X_i^*$, hence

$$\mathbb{E}(u(X^*)) = \mathbb{E}(u(X_v^*)) \ge \min_{\pi \in \Pi} \mathbb{E}(u(X_\pi^*)),$$

which concludes our proof.                                               □

Theorem 6.17 gives the following recipe for finding the optimal solution:

- find the family of state price vectors $\Pi$;
- using (6.12)–(6.13) for each $\pi \in \Pi$ compute $X_\pi^*$;
- the $X_\pi^*$ with the smallest expected utility is the candidate for the solution.

In an arbitrage free and complete model, state prices are unique, in which case finding the optimal solution turns out to be straightforward. In our setting the model is complete if the matrix $\mathbf{S}(1)$ defined in (6.1) is square (i.e. $n = N$) and invertible. Then, from (6.7), we obtain the formula for the state price vector

$$\pi^{\mathrm{T}} = \mathbf{S}(0) (\mathbf{S}(1))^{-1}. \tag{6.17}$$

By Theorem 6.7 we know that the solution to the optimisation problem exists. The state price vector $\pi$ is uniquely determined, meaning that (6.12)–(6.13) admits a unique solution $X^*$, which is the solution of the optimisation problem. Let us denote by $\mathbf{x}^*$ the strategy which gives the optimal utility,

$$X^* = V_{\mathbf{x}^*}(1).$$

Using (6.2) we can compute

$$\mathbf{x}^* = (\mathbf{S}(1))^{-1} X^*. \tag{6.18}$$

**Example 6.18**
As in Example 6.15, let us consider the problem of maximising the expected logarithmic utility. In addition to the risk-free investment and the risky asset from Example 6.15, let us also consider a second risky asset. We assume that

$$\mathbf{S}(0) = \begin{bmatrix} 1 & 100 & 200 \end{bmatrix},$$

$$\mathbf{S}(1) = \begin{bmatrix} 1 & 110 & 200 \\ 1 & 100 & 220 \\ 1 & 90 & 180 \end{bmatrix}.$$

The state prices can be computed as

$$\pi^{\mathrm{T}} = \mathbf{S}(0)\,(\mathbf{S}(1))^{-1} = \begin{bmatrix} \frac{1}{3} & \frac{1}{3} & \frac{1}{3} \end{bmatrix}.$$

Let us assume that we invest $V = 100$. From the state prices we can compute the optimal consumption using (6.14)–(6.15). Using (6.18) the optimal strategy, we obtain

$$X^* = \begin{bmatrix} 75 \\ 150 \\ 75 \end{bmatrix}, \qquad \mathbf{x}^* = \begin{bmatrix} -150 \\ -2.5 \\ 2.5 \end{bmatrix}.$$

---

**Exercise 6.6**   Consider a trinomial model $\Omega = \{\omega_1, \omega_2, \omega_3\}$, where

$$P(\{\omega_1\}) = \frac{1}{4}, \qquad P(\{\omega_2\}) = \frac{1}{2}, \qquad P(\{\omega_3\}) = \frac{1}{4},$$

with a risk-free security and a single risky asset:

$$S(0) = \begin{bmatrix} 1 & 100 \end{bmatrix},$$

$$S(1) = \begin{bmatrix} 1.02 & 120 \\ 1.02 & 110 \\ 1.02 & 90 \end{bmatrix}.$$

Find the optimal strategy, assuming that the aim of the investor is to maximise the expected utility, for the utility function $u(x) = -e^{-ax}$ with $a = 0.01$.

---

**Exercise 6.7**   Consider the trinomial model $\Omega = \{\omega_1, \omega_2, \omega_3\}$, with the same probabilities as in Exercise 6.6. Consider a risk-free security and two risky assets:

$$S(0) = \begin{bmatrix} 1 & 100 & 200 \end{bmatrix},$$

$$S(1) = \begin{bmatrix} 1.02 & 120 & 180 \\ 1.02 & 110 & 220 \\ 1.02 & 90 & 200 \end{bmatrix}.$$

Find the optimal strategy, assuming that the investor uses the same utility as in Exercise 6.6.

## 6.3   Utilities and CAPM

Our next step is to explore the relationship between utility maximisation and the Capital Asset Pricing Model.

Suppose we have $L$ investors, each aiming to maximise their own expected utility, with utility functions of the form

$$u_l(x) = a_l x - \frac{1}{2}b_l x^2,$$

where $a_l > 0$, $b_l > 0$ for $l = 1, \ldots, L$. This reflects different investment preferences for different investors. The utility function does not have to be the same for all investors.

We denote by $x_l^*$ the optimal portfolio that will be chosen by investor $l$.

The present and future total values of the market are

$$M(0) = \sum_{l=1}^{L} V_{\mathbf{x}_l^*}(0), \qquad M(1) = \sum_{l=1}^{L} V_{\mathbf{x}_l^*}(1). \qquad (6.19)$$

This is the total wealth of the investors in the market at times 0 and 1. We denote the market return by

$$K_{\mathbf{m}} = \frac{M(1) - M(0)}{M(0)}, \qquad (6.20)$$

and the risk-free return by $R$.

**Theorem 6.19**
*Assume that $M(0) \neq 0$ and $\mathrm{Var}(K_{\mathbf{m}}) \neq 0$. Then the expected return on each asset satisfies*

$$\mathbb{E}(K_j) = R + \beta_j \left( \mathbb{E}(K_{\mathbf{m}}) - R \right),$$

*for $j = 1, \dots, n$, where*

$$\beta_j = \frac{\mathrm{Cov}(K_j, K_{\mathbf{m}})}{\mathrm{Var}(K_{\mathbf{m}})}.$$

*Proof* Let the risk-free asset be designated by index $j = 1$, so that $K_1 = R$. For an investor with initial wealth $V$ and portfolio $\mathbf{x}$ we have

$$V_{\mathbf{x}}(1) = V(1 + K_{\mathbf{w}})$$

$$= V \left( 1 + \sum_{j=1}^{n} w_j K_j \right)$$

$$= V \left( 1 + \left( 1 - \sum_{j=2}^{n} w_j \right) R + \sum_{j=2}^{n} w_j K_j \right). \qquad (6.21)$$

If $\mathbf{x}_l^*$ is the optimal portfolio for investor $l$, and the initial wealth of this investor is $V_l = V_{\mathbf{x}_l^*}(0)$, then by (6.21), for $j = 2, \dots, n$, the first-order conditions for a maximum give

$$0 = \frac{\partial}{\partial w_j} \mathbb{E} \left[ u_l \left( V_{\mathbf{x}_l^*}(1) \right) \right] = V_l \mathbb{E} \left[ u_l'(V_{\mathbf{x}_l^*}(1)) \left( K_j - R \right) \right]. \qquad (6.22)$$

We use the relation $\mathrm{Cov}(X, Y) = \mathbb{E}[XY] - \mathbb{E}[X]\mathbb{E}[Y]$, which holds for any random variables $X, Y$, as $\Omega$ is finite:

$$\mathrm{Cov}\left( u_l'(V_{\mathbf{x}_l^*}(1)), K_j - R \right) = \mathbb{E} \left[ u_l'(V_{\mathbf{x}_l^*}(1)) \left( K_j - R \right) \right]$$

$$- \mathbb{E} \left[ u_l'(V_{\mathbf{x}_l^*}(1)) \right] \mathbb{E} \left[ K_j - R \right].$$

Comparing with (6.22), it follows that

$$\mathbb{E}\left[u_l'(V_{\mathbf{x}_i^*}(1))\right]\mathbb{E}\left[K_j - R\right] = -\mathrm{Cov}\left(u_l'(V_{\mathbf{x}_i^*}(1)), K_j - R\right).$$

Since $u_l'(x) = a_l - b_l x$, the above can be written as

$$\left(a_l - b_l\mathbb{E}\left[V_{\mathbf{x}_i^*}(1)\right]\right)\left(\mathbb{E}\left[K_j\right] - R\right) = -\mathrm{Cov}\left(a_l - b_l V_{\mathbf{x}_i^*}(1), K_j - R\right)$$
$$= b_l\mathrm{Cov}\left(V_{\mathbf{x}_i^*}(1), K_j\right),$$

hence

$$\left(\frac{a_l}{b_l} - \mathbb{E}\left[V_{\mathbf{x}_i^*}(1)\right]\right)\left(\mathbb{E}\left[K_j\right] - R\right) = \mathrm{Cov}\left(V_{\mathbf{x}_i^*}(1), K_j\right).$$

Taking

$$c = \sum_{l=1}^{L}\left(\frac{a_l}{b_l} - \mathbb{E}\left[V_{\mathbf{x}_i^*}(1)\right]\right),$$

summation over $l$ gives

$$
\begin{aligned}
c\left(\mathbb{E}\left[K_j\right] - R\right) &= \textstyle\sum_{l=1}^{L}\mathrm{Cov}\left(V_{\mathbf{x}_i^*}(1), K_j\right) \\
&= \mathrm{Cov}\left(M(1), K_j\right) &&\text{(by (6.19))} && (6.23) \\
&= M(0)\mathrm{Cov}\left(K_{\mathbf{m}}, K_j\right). &&\text{(by (6.20))}
\end{aligned}
$$

Let $\mathbf{m} = (m_1, \ldots, m_n)$ denote the weights of the market portfolio, then

$$
\begin{aligned}
c\left(\mathbb{E}\left[K_{\mathbf{m}}\right] - R\right) &= c\left(\mathbb{E}\left[m_1 K_1 + \cdots + m_n K_n\right] - R\right) \\
&= \sum_{j=1}^{n} cm_j\left(\mathbb{E}\left[K_j\right] - R\right) \\
&= \sum_{j=1}^{n} m_j M(0)\mathrm{Cov}\left(K_{\mathbf{m}}, K_j\right) &&\text{(by (6.23))} \\
&= M(0)\mathrm{Cov}(K_{\mathbf{m}}, K_{\mathbf{m}}) \\
&= M(0)\mathrm{Var}(K_{\mathbf{m}}).
\end{aligned}
$$

Let us observe that since $M(0) \neq 0$ and $\mathrm{Var}(K_{\mathbf{m}}) \neq 0$, the above equality implies that $c \neq 0$. As a result, combining the above with (6.23),

$$\frac{\mathbb{E}\left[K_j\right] - R}{\mathbb{E}\left[K_{\mathbf{m}}\right] - R} = \frac{\mathrm{Cov}\left(K_{\mathbf{m}}, K_j\right)}{\mathrm{Var}(K_{\mathbf{m}})} = \beta_j,$$

which completes the proof.                                                    □

Above we have shown that we can connect the mean-variance criterion for optimality of portfolios with the optimal expected utility if we assume that investors use quadratic utility functions. However, an arbitrary utility function can be approximated by a quadratic utility, if we consider its first three Taylor terms. Thus the CAPM theorem can be considered as an approximation for the optimal portfolio choice for arbitrary utility functions.

## 6.4 Risk aversion

An investor is said to be **risk averse** if

$$u(\mathbb{E}(X)) \geq \mathbb{E}(u(X)) \quad \text{for all } X \in FCS.$$

An intuitive interpretation of this inequality is that both sides represent an expected utility. On the left we have sure consumption available at the level $\mathbb{E}(X)$, on the right we are faced with an uncertain wealth $X$. The inequality says that the risk-averse investor will always choose the 'sure thing'. We say similarly that the investor is risk neutral if

$$u(\mathbb{E}(X)) = \mathbb{E}(u(X)) \quad \text{for all } X \in FCS.$$

---

**Exercise 6.8** Show that risk aversion is equivalent to $u$ being concave and illustrate the condition graphically.

---

If the investor is risk averse, we define the risk premium as a function $\gamma : FCS \to \mathbb{R}$ such that

$$u(\mathbb{E}(X) - \gamma(X)) = \mathbb{E}(u(X)).$$

The number $\mathbb{E}(X) - \gamma(X)$ is called the **certainty equivalent** of $X$. We see that an investor is indifferent between two investments $X, Y$ that have the same certainty equivalent:

$$\mathbb{E}(u(X)) = u(\mathbb{E}(X) - \gamma(X)) = u(\mathbb{E}(Y) - \gamma(Y)) = \mathbb{E}(u(Y)).$$

We shall now find an approximate formula for $\gamma$. Assume that $X$ takes values $X_1, \ldots, X_n$ (note that $n \leq N$) and that

$$P(X = X_i) = p_i.$$

Taking the second-order Taylor expansion at $X_i$ of $u$ around $m = \mathbb{E}(X)$ we obtain

$$u(X_i) \approx u(m) + u'(m)(X_i - m) + \frac{1}{2}u''(m)(X_i - m)^2.$$

Multiplying by $p_i$ and summing we get

$$\mathbb{E}(u(X)) \approx u(m) + u'(m)\mathbb{E}(X - m) + \frac{1}{2}u''(m)\mathbb{E}(X - m)^2 \qquad (6.24)$$

$$= u(m) + \frac{1}{2}u''(m)\text{Var}(X).$$

Taking the first-order Taylor expansion of $u$ at $m - \gamma(X)$ around $m$ gives

$$u(m - \gamma(X)) \approx u(m) - u'(m)\gamma(X),$$

so (by the definition of the risk premium)

$$\mathbb{E}(u(X)) = u(m - \gamma(X)) \approx u(m) - u'(m)\gamma(X). \qquad (6.25)$$

Comparing the right-hand sides of (6.24) and (6.25) we get

$$u(m) + \frac{1}{2}u''(m)\text{Var}(X) \approx u(m) - u'(m)\gamma(X),$$

which yields

$$\gamma(X) \approx -\frac{1}{2}\frac{u''(\mathbb{E}(X))}{u'(\mathbb{E}(X))}\text{Var}(X).$$

The number

$$ARA = -\frac{u''(\mathbb{E}(X))}{u'(\mathbb{E}(X))}$$

is called the **absolute risk aversion** coefficient.

The above discussion was formulated in terms of wealth. We can reformulate the result in terms of returns. Let $X = V(1 + K)$, where $V$ is the initial investment and $K$ is the return with expectation $\mu$ and variance $\sigma^2$. Using the fact that

$$\mathbb{E}(X) = \mathbb{E}(V(1 + K)) = V(1 + \mu), \qquad (6.26)$$
$$\text{Var}(X) = \text{Var}(V(1 + K)) = V^2\sigma^2,$$

the risk premium is approximated using

$$\gamma(X) \approx -\frac{V^2}{2}\frac{u''(V(1 + \mu))}{u'(V(1 + \mu))}\sigma^2. \qquad (6.27)$$

An investor is indifferent to the choice between securities with the same certainty equivalent. Looking at the $(\sigma, \mu)$-plane, by (6.26)–(6.27), the certainty equivalent can be approximated in terms of an indifference curve

$$\mathbb{E}(X) - \gamma(X) \approx V(1 + \mu) - \frac{V^2}{2} \frac{u''(V(1 + \mu))}{u'(V(1 + \mu))} \sigma^2.$$

**Example 6.20**
Assume that an investor has an exponential utility $u(x) = -e^{-ax}$. Then

$$u'(x) = ae^{-ax}, \qquad u''(x) = -a^2 e^{-ax},$$

which means that absolute risk aversion coefficient is constant

$$ARA = -\frac{u''(\mathbb{E}(X))}{u'(\mathbb{E}(X))} = a.$$

The certainty equivalent of $X$ is then

$$\mathbb{E}(X) - \gamma(X) = V\left[\mu - \frac{aV}{2}\sigma^2\right] + V. \tag{6.28}$$

This yields the same type of indifference curve as considered in Example 2.13.

---

**Exercise 6.9** Based on the data from Exercise 6.7 compute $\mu_1$, $\mu_2$, $\sigma_1$, $\sigma_2$ and $\rho_{12}$. Find the expected return and standard deviation of the market portfolio. Consider indifference curves given by (6.28). Following the method from Example 2.13, find the point on the $(\sigma, \mu)$-plane, which has the highest certainty equivalent.

---

**Exercise 6.10** Find the weights of the portfolio computed in Exercise 6.9. Based on these compute the strategy which has the highest certainty equivalent. Compare the result with the solution of Exercise 6.7, where we have found the optimal strategy which maximises the expected utility. Explain why the two are not the same.

# 7

## Value at Risk

Until now we have focused our attention on variance, or equivalently, standard deviation of the return, as a tool for measuring risk. The standard deviation measures the spread of the random future return from its mean. In portfolio selection we seek to minimise the variance while maximising the return. However, an investor, seeking to measure the risk inherent in an asset he holds, is naturally more concerned to place a bound on his potential losses, while remaining relaxed about possible high levels of profit. Thus one looks for risk measures which focus on the downside risk, that is, measures concerned with the lower tail of the distribution of the return. Variance and standard deviation are symmetric, so they are not good candidates in this search.

In looking for quantitative measures of the overall risk in a portfolio, we seek a statistic which can be applied universally, enabling us to compare the risks of different types of risky portfolio. Ideally, we look for a number (or set of numbers) that expresses the potential loss with a given level of confidence, enabling the risk manager to adjudge the risk as acceptable or not.

In the wake of spectacular financial collapses in the early 1990s at Barings Bank and Orange County, **Value at Risk** (henceforth abbreviated as VaR) became a standard benchmark for measuring financial risk. It has the advantage of relative simplicity and ease of use when sufficient data are available. Its principal drawback is that it does not provide information about the potential impact of extreme (i.e. highly unlikely) events. In this chapter we explore this popular risk measure. Our focus is on its computation, for discrete, continuous and mixed distributions, and this will highlight a further defect, showing that VaR for a diversified position can be higher than for investment in a single asset.

In the final section we give a detailed analysis, in a Black–Scholes context, of hedging to minimise VaR with the judicious use of European put options.

## 7.1 Quantiles

An investor holding an asset whose future value is uncertain may wish to determine whether his discounted gain $X$ on an investment has at least 95% probability of remaining above a certain (usually negative) level. Value at Risk at 5% answers this question by specifying the minimum loss incurred in the worst 5% of possible outcomes. Its calculation is therefore closely tied to the values of the distribution function $F_X$ of $X$. This leads us to examine the so-called quantiles of $F_X$ more closely.

We begin with a simple example.

**Example 7.1**
Consider a two step binomial model with stock prices

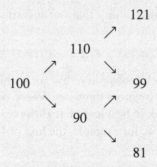

Assume that the probability $p$ of the price going up in a single step is $p = 0.8$. In this example we neglect the time value of money and compute the gain after the second step of buying a single share of stock as

$$X = S(2) - S(0),$$

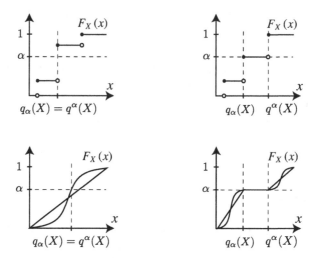

**Figure 7.1** The upper and lower quantiles for various distribution functions.

which gives

$$X = \begin{cases} 21 & \text{with probability } p^2 = 0.64, \\ -1 & \text{with probability } 2p(1-p) = 0.32, \\ -19 & \text{with probability } (1-p)^2 = 0.04. \end{cases}$$

We can see that the probability that our investment will lead to a loss $L = -X < 19$ is

$$P(L < 19) = P(X > -19) = 0.96.$$

This means that with with probability 96% we will lose no more than 1. If we agree, for instance, to ignore the worst 5% of potential outcomes, our 'worst-case scenario' would be a loss of 1. However, if we are only willing to exclude the worst 2.5%, for example, the loss of 19 should be taken into account.

An outcome at a given probability can be expressed using quantiles.

Let $(\Omega, \mathcal{F}, P)$ be a probability space and let $X : \Omega \to \mathbb{R}$ be a random variable. The cumulative distribution function $F_X : \mathbb{R} \to [0, 1]$, defined by $F_X(x) = P(X \leq x)$ is right-continuous and non-decreasing (see [PF] for details).

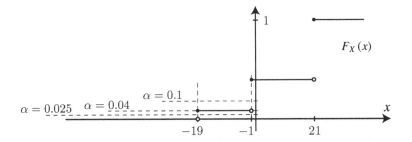

**Figure 7.2** The plot of the distribution function from Example 7.1.

**Definition 7.2**
For $\alpha \in (0, 1)$ the number

$$q^{\alpha}(X) = \inf\{x : \alpha < F_X(x)\}, \qquad (7.1)$$

is called the **upper $\alpha$-quantile** of $X$. The number

$$q_{\alpha}(X) = \inf\{x : \alpha \le F_X(x)\}, \qquad (7.2)$$

is called the **lower $\alpha$-quantile** of $X$. Any

$$q \in [q_{\alpha}(X), q^{\alpha}(X)],$$

is called an **$\alpha$-quantile** of $X$.

The definition is best understood when looking at the graph of the cumulative distribution function. In Figure 7.1 we can see that the upper and the lower quantiles differ when the plot of $F_X(x)$ becomes flat at the value $F_X(x) = \alpha$, otherwise they are equal.

**Example 7.3**
For $X$ from Example 7.1 we can compute the upper and the lower $\alpha$-quantiles, for $\alpha \in \{0.025, 0.04, 0.1\}$, as (see Figure 7.2)

$$q^{0.025}(X) = -19, \qquad q_{0.025}(X) = -19,$$
$$q^{0.04}(X) = -1, \qquad q_{0.04}(X) = -19,$$
$$q^{0.1}(X) = -1, \qquad q_{0.1}(X) = -1.$$

We list some basic properties of quantiles. The proofs are all elementary, but we defer the more technical parts to the end of the chapter to avoid disturbing the flow of development.

**Proposition 7.4**

*Let X, Y be random variables.*
  (i) *$X \geq Y$ implies $q^{\alpha}(X) \geq q^{\alpha}(Y)$.*
  (ii) *For any $b \in \mathbb{R}$, $q^{\alpha}(X + b) = q^{\alpha}(X) + b$.*
 (iii) *For $b > 0$, $q^{\alpha}(bX) = bq^{\alpha}(X)$.*
 (iv) *$q^{\alpha}(-X) = -q_{1-\alpha}(X)$.*

*Proof*  See page 120.                                    □

**Lemma 7.5**

*If $F_X(x)$ is continuous and strictly increasing then*

$$q^{\alpha}(X) = F_X^{-1}(\alpha).$$

*Proof*  The given conditions on $F_X$ ensure that it is invertible, the inverse function $\alpha \to F^{-1}(\alpha)$ is continuous, and $\alpha < F_X(x)$ is equivalent to $F_X^{-1}(\alpha) < x$. This gives

$$q^{\alpha}(X) = \inf\{x : \alpha < F_X(x)\} = \inf\{x : F_X^{-1}(\alpha) < x\} = F_X^{-1}(\alpha),$$

which concludes our proof.                                    □

**Lemma 7.6**

*Let X be a random variable. If $f : \mathbb{R} \to \mathbb{R}$ is right-continuous and non-decreasing then*

$$q^{\alpha}(f(X)) = f(q^{\alpha}(X)).$$

*Proof*  See page 122.                                    □

---

**Exercise 7.1**  Formulate and prove mirror results to Proposition 7.4 and Lemmas 7.5 and 7.6 for lower $\alpha$-quantiles.

---

## 7.2  Measuring downside risk

We work in a single-step financial market model in which we invest at time $t = 0$ and terminate our investment at $t = T$. We denote by $X$ the discounted value of the investor's position at time $T$.

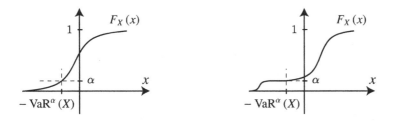

**Figure 7.3** $-\text{VaR}^{\alpha}(X)$ is the upper $\alpha$-quantile for $X$.

**Definition 7.7**
For $\alpha$ in $(0, 1)$, we define the **Value at Risk** (VaR) of $X$, at confidence level $1 - \alpha$, as (see Figure 7.3)

$$\text{VaR}^{\alpha}(X) = -q^{\alpha}(X) = -\inf\{x : \alpha < F_X(x)\}.$$

To gain some intuition, let us consider the following example.

**Example 7.8**
Let $X$ be as in Example 7.1. By looking at the distribution function $F_X(x)$ (see Figure 7.2) we can see that

$$\text{VaR}^{0.04}(X) = 1,$$
$$\text{VaR}^{0.025}(X) = 19.$$

Let us observe that since $X$ denotes the gain from an investment, $-X$ denotes the loss. We can express VaR in terms of the loss as follows:

$$\begin{aligned}
\text{VaR}^{\alpha}(X) &= -q^{\alpha}(X) \\
&= q_{1-\alpha}(-X) \qquad \text{(by (iv) from Proposition 7.4)} \\
&= \inf\{x : 1 - \alpha \le P(-X \le x)\} \\
&= \inf\{x : P(x < -X) \le \alpha\}.
\end{aligned}$$

In loose terms, this means that the probability of the loss exceeding $\text{VaR}^{\alpha}$ is no greater than $\alpha$. In other words, at confidence level $1 - \alpha$, our loss is no worse than $\text{VaR}^{\alpha}$.

Simple algebraic properties of VaR follow from those we proved for the upper quantile:

**Proposition 7.9**
*Let X, Y be random variables.*
  (i) $X \geq Y$ *implies* $\text{VaR}^{\alpha}(X) \leq \text{VaR}^{\alpha}(Y)$,
 (ii) *For any* $a \in \mathbb{R}$, $\text{VaR}^{\alpha}(X + a) = \text{VaR}^{\alpha}(X) - a$,
(iii) *For any* $a \geq 0$, $\text{VaR}^{\alpha}(aX) = a\text{VaR}^{\alpha}(X)$.

*Proof* The proof follows from the properties of quantiles proved in Proposition 7.4, and is left as an exercise.                                                       □

---

**Exercise 7.2**   Prove Proposition 7.9.

---

## 7.3  Computing VaR: examples

To familiarise ourselves with the definition of VaR let us consider a few simple examples.

We shall assume that at time zero we invest $V(0)$ to receive $V(T)$ at time $T$. We use $X$ to denote the discounted gain at time $T$

$$X = e^{-rT} V(T) - V(0),$$

where $r$ is the risk-free rate for continuous compounding.

**Example 7.10**
Suppose that we invest $V(0)$ risk-free. Then $V(T) = e^{rT} V(0)$, giving

$$X = e^{-rT} V(T) - V(0) = 0.$$

The distribution function of $X$ is then

$$F_X(x) = \begin{cases} 1 & \text{for } x \geq 0, \\ 0 & \text{for } x < 0. \end{cases}$$

For any $\alpha \in (0, 1)$, $q^{\alpha}(X) = 0$, which gives

$$\text{VaR}^{\alpha}(X) = -q^{\alpha}(X) = 0.$$

> **Exercise 7.3** For the leveraged stockholding described in Exercise 1.5, compare the VaR of the discounted gain for the leveraged position with that of the stock.

**Example 7.11**

Consider

$$X = \begin{cases} -20 & \text{with probability } 0.025, \\ -10 & \text{with probability } 0.025, \end{cases} \tag{7.3}$$

and $P(X > 0) = 0.95$. For $x < 0$

$$F_X(x) = \begin{cases} 0 & x \in (-\infty, -20), \\ 0.025 & x \in [-20, -10), \\ 0.05 & x \in [-10, 0). \end{cases}$$

Taking $\alpha = 0.05$ we have

$$\text{VaR}^{0.05}(X) = -q^{0.05}(X) = 10.$$

For any $\alpha < 0.05$,

$$\text{VaR}^{\alpha}(X) = -q^{\alpha}(X) = 20,$$

which demonstrates that $\text{VaR}^{\alpha}$ can be sensitive to the choice of $\alpha$.

Let us now change the value $-20$ in (7.3) to $-2000$. The $\text{VaR}^{0.05}$ still remains equal to 10! This illustrates that VaR does not take into consideration unlikely events (i.e. with probability below the chosen threshold $\alpha$), whatever the severity of their outcome. This is an undesirable feature in a risk measure.

**Example 7.12**

Consider two independent investments $X_1, X_2$ with gains

$$X_i = \begin{cases} 0 & \text{with probability } p, \\ 1 & \text{with probability } 1 - p, \end{cases}$$

for $i = 1, 2$. We can think of these as corporate bonds with the same price and maturity date, of two independent companies that each have a probability of default with zero recovery equal to $p$.

If $p < \alpha$ then

$$\text{VaR}^\alpha(X_1) = \text{VaR}^\alpha(X_2) = 0.$$

If, instead, we buy half a unit of each of the two bonds, then our gain will be equal to

$$\frac{1}{2}X_1 + \frac{1}{2}X_2 = \begin{cases} 0 & \text{with probability } p^2, \\ \frac{1}{2} & \text{with probability } 2p(1 - p), \\ 1 & \text{with probability } (1 - p)^2. \end{cases}$$

If we choose $\alpha \in (p, p^2 + 2p(1 - p))$ then

$$F_{\frac{1}{2}X_1 + \frac{1}{2}X_2}\left(\frac{1}{2}\right) = p^2 + 2p(1 - p) > \alpha$$

hence

$$\text{VaR}^\alpha\left(\frac{1}{2}X_1 + \frac{1}{2}X_2\right) = \frac{1}{2}.$$

We can see that

$$\text{VaR}^\alpha\left(\frac{1}{2}X_1 + \frac{1}{2}X_2\right) > \max\{\text{VaR}^\alpha(X_1), \text{VaR}^\alpha(X_2)\},$$

which means that the risk of a diversified position, as measured by VaR, is greater than the risk of investing all our funds in a single bond. This runs counter to the principle that diversification should reduce risk, and therefore illustrates a second serious drawback in using VaR to measure risk. In the next chapter we will consider risk measures designed to remedy these defects.

From examples explored so far we see that finding VaR in the case of discrete distributions is an easy task. This is summarised in the following lemma.

**Lemma 7.13**
*Assume that $X$ is a discrete random variable with $P(X = x_i) = p_i$, $\sum_{i=1}^{N} p_i = 1$, and $x_1 < x_2 < \cdots < x_N$. Then*

$$\text{VaR}^\alpha(X) = -x_{k_\alpha},$$

*where $k_\alpha \in \mathbb{N}$ is the largest number such that $\sum_{i=1}^{k_\alpha - 1} p_i \leq \alpha$.*

*Proof* Since $X$ has discrete distribution and $x_1 < x_2 < \ldots < x_N$ we can see that

$$P(X \leq x_k) = \sum_{i=1}^{k} p_i. \qquad (7.4)$$

We shall also use the fact that

$$\min\{k : \alpha < \sum_{i=1}^{k} p_i\} = \max\{k : \sum_{i=1}^{k-1} p_i \leq \alpha\}. \qquad (7.5)$$

This gives

$$
\begin{aligned}
q^\alpha(X) &= \inf\{x : \alpha < P(X \leq x)\} && \text{(by (7.1))}\\
&= \min\{x_k : \alpha < P(X \leq x_k)\} && \text{(since } X \in \{x_1, \ldots, x_N\})\\
&= \min\{x_k : \alpha < \sum_{i=1}^{k} p_i\} && \text{(by (7.4))}\\
&= \max\{x_k : \sum_{i=1}^{k-1} p_i \leq \alpha\} && \text{(by (7.5))}\\
&= x_{k_\alpha} && \text{(by definition of } k_\alpha).
\end{aligned}
$$

This concludes our proof, since $\mathrm{VaR}^\alpha(X) = -q^\alpha(X)$. $\qquad\square$

We now turn to the computation of VaR for random variables with continuous distributions. For a standard normal random variable $Z$, with distribution function $N(x) = \frac{1}{\sqrt{2\pi}} \int_{-\infty}^{x} e^{-\frac{z^2}{2}} dz$, Lemma 7.5 yields

$$\mathrm{VaR}^\alpha(Z) = -N^{-1}(\alpha)$$

for any $\alpha \in (0, 1)$. We use this in the next example.

**Example 7.14**
Suppose that today's price of the stock is equal to $S(0)$. Assume also that the price of the stock at time $T$ is equal to $S(T) = S(0)e^{m+\sigma Z}$, with $Z$ having standard normal distribution $N(0, 1)$. We shall compute $\mathrm{VaR}^\alpha(X)$ for

$$X = e^{-rT}S(T) - S(0).$$

By Lemma 7.5, $q^\alpha(Z) = N^{-1}(\alpha)$, where $N$ is the standard normal cumulative distribution function. Observing that

$$X = f(Z),$$

where

$$f(\zeta) = e^{-rT} S(0) e^{m+\sigma\zeta} - S(0)$$

is an increasing function,

$$\begin{aligned}
\text{VaR}^\alpha(X) &= -q^\alpha(f(Z)) \\
&= -f(q^\alpha(Z)) && \text{(by Lemma 7.6)} \\
&= -f(N^{-1}(\alpha)) && \text{(by Lemma 7.5)} \\
&= S(0)\left(1 - e^{m-rT+\sigma N^{-1}(\alpha)}\right).
\end{aligned} \qquad (7.6)$$

In Example 7.14 we have exploited the fact that $X$ was a non-decreasing function of a random variable with standard normal distribution, for which quantiles are easy to compute. This idea can be formulated in more general terms as follows.

**Lemma 7.15**

*Let $f : \mathbb{R} \to \mathbb{R}$ be a non-decreasing right-continuous function. Then*

$$\text{VaR}^\alpha(f(X)) = -f(q^\alpha(X)).$$

*Proof* By Lemma 7.6

$$\text{VaR}^\alpha(f(X)) = -q^\alpha(f(X)) = -f(q^\alpha(X)),$$

which concludes our proof. □

We now show that VaR can be computed using Monte Carlo simulations. First we need some auxiliary results.

For a sequence of random variables $\{Y_i\}_{i=1}^\infty$ we write $Y_i \xrightarrow{P} Y$ to denote that $Y_i$ converges to $Y$ in probability. (See [PF] for details of the standard results and terminology from probability we use here.)

**Lemma 7.16**

*Let $X_1, X_2, \ldots$ be a sequence of i.i.d. random variables, $X_i : \Omega \to \mathbb{R}$, with the same distribution as $X$. Let $x \in \mathbb{R}$ be fixed. If we take a sequence of random variables $F_N(x) : \Omega \to \mathbb{R}$ defined as*

$$F_N(x) = \frac{1}{N} \sum_{i=1}^N 1_{\{X_i \le x\}},$$

*then $F_N(x) \xrightarrow{P} F_X(x)$.*

*Proof* Let us introduce the following notation: $Y_i = 1_{\{X_i \leq x\}}$ and $Y = 1_{\{X \leq x\}}$. By the weak law of large numbers (see [PF]), $\frac{1}{N} \sum_{i=1}^{N} Y_i \xrightarrow{P} \mathbb{E}(Y)$, hence

$$F_N(x) = \frac{1}{N} \sum_{i=1}^{N} Y_i \xrightarrow{P} \mathbb{E}(Y) = \mathbb{E}\left(1_{\{X \leq x\}}\right) = P(X \leq x) = F_X(x),$$

as required. □

Suppose now that $\hat{X}_1, \ldots, \hat{X}_N$ are results of simulations following the same distribution as $X$ and let

$$\hat{F}_N(x) = \frac{1}{N} \sum_{i=1}^{N} 1_{\{\hat{X}_i \leq x\}}.$$

By Lemma 7.16, for any $x \in \mathbb{R}$,

$$F_X(x) = \lim_{N \to \infty} \hat{F}_N(x). \tag{7.7}$$

Let $Y_N$ denote the discrete random variable with distribution

$$P(Y_N = \hat{X}_i) = \frac{1}{N} \qquad \text{for } i = 1, \ldots, N.$$

The distribution function $F_{Y_N}$ is equal to $\hat{F}_N$. By (7.7), taking sufficiently large $N$, $\text{VaR}^\alpha(X)$ can be approximated using $\text{VaR}^\alpha(Y_N)$,

$$\text{VaR}^\alpha(X) \approx \text{VaR}^\alpha(Y_N). \tag{7.8}$$

The $\text{VaR}^\alpha(Y_N)$ can easily be computed using Lemma 7.13. We shall implement this method in the following section, to compute VaR in the $n$-dimensional Black–Scholes market (see Example 7.24).

## 7.4 VaR in the Black–Scholes model

In the **Black–Scholes model** we have a single stock and a risk-free asset. The time zero price of the stock is $S(0) > 0$. The stock price at time $T$ is given by

$$S(T) = S(0)e^{\left(\mu - \frac{\sigma^2}{2}\right)T + \sigma \sqrt{T} Z}, \tag{7.9}$$

where $\mu$ and $\sigma$ are positive real parameters, and $Z$ is a random variable with standard normal distribution $N(0, 1)$. The parameter $\mu$ represents the **drift** and the parameter $\sigma$ represents the **volatility** of the stock. The risk-free rate is constant and equal to $r > 0$, with continuous compounding, meaning that the time $T$ price of the risk-free asset is

$$A(T) = A(0)e^{rT}. \tag{7.10}$$

For simplicity, we assume that

$$A(0) = 1.$$

A **European put option** with **strike price** $K$ and maturity $T$ has payoff

$$(K - S(T))^+ = \max(K - S(T), 0),$$

and costs

$$P(r, T, K, S(0), \sigma) = Ke^{-rT}N(-d_-) - S(0)N(-d_+), \tag{7.11}$$

where

$$d_+ = \frac{\ln \frac{S(0)}{K} + \left(r + \frac{1}{2}\sigma^2\right)T}{\sigma\sqrt{T}}, \qquad d_- = \frac{\ln \frac{S(0)}{K} + \left(r - \frac{1}{2}\sigma^2\right)T}{\sigma\sqrt{T}}, \tag{7.12}$$

and $N$ is the standard normal cumulative distribution function. For more details on the Black–Scholes model see [BSM].

Let $H(t)$ denote the value of a put option at time $t = 0, T$

$$H(0) = P(r, T, K, S(0), \sigma),$$
$$H(T) = (K - S(T))^+. \tag{7.13}$$

We start with a simple lemma.

**Lemma 7.17**
*For $S(T)$ and $H(T)$ given by (7.9) and (7.13), respectively,*

$$q^\alpha(S(T)) = S(0)e^{\left(\mu - \frac{\sigma^2}{2}\right)T + \sigma\sqrt{T}N^{-1}(\alpha)}, \tag{7.14}$$

$$q^\alpha(-H(T)) = -(K - q^\alpha(S(T)))^+. \tag{7.15}$$

*Proof* By Lemma 7.5, $q^\alpha(Z) = N^{-1}(\alpha)$. Since $z \longmapsto S(0)e^{(\mu - \frac{\sigma^2}{2})T + \sigma\sqrt{T}z}$ is an increasing function, (7.14) follows from Lemma 7.6.

Similarly, since $\zeta \longmapsto -(K - \zeta)^+$ is a non-decreasing function, (7.15) also follows from Lemma 7.6. □

Assume that we buy a single share of stock. The discounted gain from this investment is

$$X = e^{-rT}S(T) - S(0).$$

By Lemma 7.15 we can see that

$$\text{VaR}^\alpha(X) = S(0) - e^{-rT} q^\alpha(S(T)). \tag{7.16}$$

---

**Exercise 7.4** Compute $\text{VaR}^{5\%}(X)$ for an investment in a stock with parameters $S(0) = 100, \mu = 10\%, \sigma = 0.2, r = 3\%$ and $T = 1$.

---

We now consider an investment where at time zero we buy $x$ shares of stock and $y$ units of the risk-free asset. For $t = 0, T$ we use $V_{(x,y)}(t)$ to denote the value of the portfolio at time $t$

$$V_{(x,y)}(t) = xS(t) + yA(t).$$

We use $X_{(x,y)}$ to denote the discounted gain

$$X_{(x,y)} = e^{-rT} V_{(x,y)}(T) - V_{(x,y)}(0).$$

**Lemma 7.18**
*If $x \geq 0$ then*

$$\text{VaR}^\alpha\left(X_{(x,y)}\right) = V_{(x,y)}(0) - xe^{-rT} q^\alpha(S(T)) - y. \tag{7.17}$$

*Proof* Since $x \geq 0$, the discounted gain can be expressed as a non-decreasing function of $S(T)$ :

$$X_{(x,y)} = f(S(T)),$$

with

$$\begin{aligned} f(\zeta) &= e^{-rT} (x\zeta + yA(T)) - V_{(x,y)}(0) \\ &= e^{-rT} x\zeta + y - V_{(x,y)}(0), \end{aligned}$$

hence (7.17) follows from Lemma 7.15. □

Choosing any $x \in (0, 1)$ and $y = (1 - x)S(0)$ we can see that the initial value of the investment is

$$V_{(x,y)}(0) = S(0).$$

Let $\text{VaR}^\alpha(X)$ be the Value at Risk for the investment in a single unit of stock, given in (7.16). Then

$$\begin{aligned} \text{VaR}^\alpha\left(X_{(x,y)}\right) &= V_{(x,y)}(0) - xe^{-rT} q^\alpha(S(T)) - y && \text{(from (7.17))} \\ &= xS(0) - xe^{-rT} q^\alpha(S(T)) && (V_{(x,y)}(0) = xS(0) + y) \\ &= x\text{VaR}^\alpha(X) && \text{(from (7.16))} \\ &< \text{VaR}^\alpha(X). \end{aligned}$$

This means that diversifying an investment between the stock and the risk-free asset reduces VaR (which is hardly a surprise!).

---

**Exercise 7.5** Derive the formula for $\mathbb{E}(X_{(x,y)})$. Taking the values $S(0)$, $\mu, \sigma, r$ and $T$ as in Exercise 7.4, plot the set

$$\left\{\left(\text{VaR}^\alpha(X_{(x,y)}), \mathbb{E}(X_{(x,y)})\right) : x \in [0, 1], y = (1-x)S(0)\right\}.$$

---

**Exercise 7.6** Consider buying $x > 0$ shares of stock and entering into $\theta \in [0, x]$ forward contracts to sell the stock at time $T$ for the forward price $F = S(0)e^{rT}$. Let

$$X_{(x,\theta)} = xe^{-rT}S(T) + \theta e^{-rT}(F - S(T)) - xS(0)$$

denote the discounted gain of such an investment. Derive formulae for $\mathbb{E}(X_{(x,\theta)})$ and $\text{VaR}^\alpha(X_{(x,\theta)})$.

Taking the values $S(0), \mu, \sigma, r$ and $T$ as in Exercise 7.4, plot the set

$$\{(\text{VaR}^\alpha(X_{(x,\theta)}), \mathbb{E}(X_{(x,\theta)})) : x = 1, \theta \in [0, 1]\},$$

and compare with the plot obtained in Exercise 7.5. Which is more efficient, reducing VaR with bonds or with forward contracts?

---

Another natural idea to reduce VaR is to buy European put options. By doing so one can protect against undesirable scenarios, while leaving oneself open to the positive outcomes. Assume that at time zero we buy $x$ units of stock and $z$ put options with strike price $K$. The value of such an investment is

$$V_{(x,z)}(t) = xS(t) + zH(t),$$

and the discounted gain is

$$\begin{aligned} X_{(x,z)} &= e^{-rT}V_{(x,z)}(T) - V_{(x,z)}(0) \\ &= e^{-rT}\left(xS(T) + z(K - S(T))^+\right) - V_{(x,z)}(0). \end{aligned}$$

**Lemma 7.19**

*If $0 < z \le x$ then*

$$\text{VaR}^\alpha(X_{(x,z)}) = V_{(x,z)}(0) - e^{-rT}\left(xq^\alpha(S(T)) + z(K - q^\alpha(S(T)))^+\right). \quad (7.18)$$

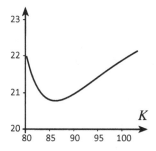

**Figure 7.4** $\text{VaR}^{5\%}\left(X_{(x,z(K))}\right)$ for different choices of $K$, for parameters $V_0 = S(0) = 100$, $\mu = 0.1$, $\sigma = 0.2$, $r = 0.03$, $T = 1$ and $x = 0.99$.

*Proof* Since $0 < z \le x$, we see that $X_{(x,z)}$ can be expressed as a non-decreasing function of $S(T)$,

$$X_{(x,z)} = f(S(T)),$$

with

$$f(\zeta) = e^{-rT}\left(x\zeta + z(K - \zeta)^+\right) - V_{(x,z)}(0).$$

By Lemma 7.15

$$\begin{aligned}
\text{VaR}^\alpha\left(X_{(x,z)}\right) &= -f\left(q^\alpha(S(T))\right) \\
&= e^{-rT}\left(-xq^\alpha(S(T)) - z(K - q^\alpha(S(T)))^+\right) + V_{(x,z)}(0),
\end{aligned}$$

which combined with (7.15) gives (7.18).      □

**Example 7.20**
Assume that we want to invest $V_0$ at time zero and buy $x$ shares of stock. In order to have $V_{(x,z)}(0) = V_0$ we need to buy

$$z = z(K) = \frac{V_0 - xS(0)}{P(r, T, K, S(0), \sigma)}$$

put options. Depending on the choice of the strike price $K$ we obtain different values of

$$\text{VaR}^\alpha\left(X_{(x,z(K))}\right) = V_0 - e^{-rT}\left(xq^\alpha(S(T)) + z(K)(K - q^\alpha(S(T)))^+\right)$$

(see Figure 7.4).

The choice of a high strike price makes the term $(K - q^\alpha(S(T)))^+$ large, but since options with a high strike prices are expensive, their number

$z(K)$ is small. On the other hand, if we choose a low strike price, then we can buy a larger number $z(K)$ of options, but each offers lower payoff $(K - q^\alpha(S(T)))^+$. An optimal choice of the strike price $K$ lies somewhere between these extremes (see Figure 7.4).

---

**Exercise 7.7** Let $V_0 = S(0) = 100$, $\mu = 10\%$, $\sigma = 0.2$, $r = 3\%$, $T = 1$ and $x = 0.99$. Find $K$ which minimises $\text{VaR}^\alpha (X_{(x,z(K))})$.

---

Usually we do not have full freedom of choice for the strike price of a put option and need to choose between options which are available on the market. Let us assume that we can invest in $n$ put options with strike prices $K_1, \ldots, K_n$ and maturity $T$. We denote by $H_i(t)$ the payoff of a put option with strike price $K_i$; in particular

$$H_i(0) = P(r, T, K_i, S(0), \sigma),$$
$$H_i(T) = (K_i - S(T))^+ .$$

Assume that we buy $x$ shares of stock and $z_i$ put options with strike prices $K_i$, for $i = 1, \ldots, n$. Let $\mathbf{z}$, $\mathbf{1}$ and $\mathbf{H}(t)$ for $t = 0, T$ be vectors in $\mathbb{R}^n$ defined as

$$\mathbf{z} = \begin{bmatrix} z_1 \\ \vdots \\ z_n \end{bmatrix}, \qquad \mathbf{1} = \begin{bmatrix} 1 \\ \vdots \\ 1 \end{bmatrix}, \qquad \mathbf{H}(t) = \begin{bmatrix} H_1(t) \\ \vdots \\ H_n(t) \end{bmatrix}.$$

The value of our investment at time $t$ is

$$V_{(x,\mathbf{z})}(t) = xS(t) + \mathbf{z}^T \mathbf{H}(t).$$

We show how to compute VaR for

$$X_{(x,\mathbf{z})} = e^{-rT} V_{(x,\mathbf{z})}(T) - V_{(x,\mathbf{z})}(0).$$

**Proposition 7.21**

*If $z_i \geq 0$, for $i = 1, \ldots, n$, and $\sum_{i=1}^{n} z_i = \mathbf{z}^T \mathbf{1} \leq x$, then*

$$\text{VaR}^\alpha (X_{(x,\mathbf{z})}) = V_{(x,\mathbf{z})}(0) - e^{-rT} \left( xq^\alpha(S(T)) - \mathbf{z}^T q^\alpha(-\mathbf{H}(T)) \right), \qquad (7.19)$$

*where*

$$q^\alpha(-\mathbf{H}(T)) = -\begin{bmatrix} (K_1 - q^\alpha(S(T)))^+ \\ \vdots \\ (K_n - q^\alpha(S(T)))^+ \end{bmatrix}. \tag{7.20}$$

*Proof* The formula (7.20) follows from Lemma 7.17.

Since $\mathbf{z}^\mathsf{T}\mathbf{1} \le x$, the function

$$\zeta \longmapsto e^{-rT}\left(x\zeta + \sum_{i=1}^n z_i (K_i - \zeta)^+\right) - V_{(x,\mathbf{z})}(0)$$

is non-decreasing, which by Lemma 7.6 implies that

$$\text{VaR}^\alpha(X_{(x,\mathbf{z})}) = V_{(x,\mathbf{z})}(0) - e^{-rT}\left(xq^\alpha(S(T)) + \sum_{i=1}^n z_i (K_i - q^\alpha(S(T)))^+\right),$$

and this is (7.19).  □

From now on we shall assume that $x$ is fixed and investigate how to minimise $\text{VaR}^\alpha(X_{(x,\mathbf{z})})$ by choosing $\mathbf{z}$. We assume that we have $V_0$ at our disposal for investment and hedging purposes. This means that we spend

$$c = V_0 - xS(0)$$

on put options. We assume that we do not take short positions in stock or puts, and that the number of options does not exceed the number of shares of stock in our portfolio. These restrictions are imposed by common sense. (Later in this chapter we give an example of what might happen if these are violated.) Under such assumptions, by (7.19), minimising $\text{VaR}^\alpha(X_{(x,\mathbf{z})})$ is equivalent to the following problem:

$$\begin{aligned} &\min \mathbf{z}^\mathsf{T} q^\alpha(-\mathbf{H}(T)), \\ &\text{subject to:} \quad \mathbf{z}^\mathsf{T}\mathbf{H}(0) = c, \\ &\qquad\qquad\quad \mathbf{z}^\mathsf{T}\mathbf{1} \le x, \\ &\qquad\qquad\quad z_0, \dots, z_n \ge 0. \end{aligned} \tag{7.21}$$

Since $\mathbf{H}(0)$ and $q^\alpha(-\mathbf{H}(T))$ are fixed vectors in $\mathbb{R}^n$, (7.21) is a typical linear programming problem, which can be solved numerically.

**Example 7.22**
Consider the Black–Scholes model with parameters $S(0) = 100$, $\mu = 10\%$, $\sigma = 0.2$ and $r = 3\%$. Assume that we want to invest $V_0 = 1000$ in stock and put options with strike prices $K_1 = 75$, $K_2 = 90$, $K_3 = 110$ with

expiry $T = 1$. We shall solve the problem (7.21) for $\alpha = 0.05$, considering $c = 0, 10, 30, 50$ and 80.

We compute the prices of the put options using (7.11)

$$\mathbf{H}(0) = \begin{bmatrix} 0.406 \\ 2.769 \\ 12.042 \end{bmatrix}.$$

Using the fact that $N^{-1}(0.05) = -1.645$ we compute

$$q^{\alpha}(S(T)) = S(0)e^{(\mu - \frac{\sigma^2}{2})T + \sigma\sqrt{T}N^{-1}(\alpha)} = 77.96$$

and

$$q^{\alpha}(-\mathbf{H}(T)) = \begin{bmatrix} 0 \\ -12.04 \\ -32.04 \end{bmatrix}.$$

The numerical solutions of (7.21) are given in the table below.

| $c$ | $x$ | $z_1$ | $z_2$ | $z_3$ | VaR$^{\alpha}$ |
|-----|-----|-------|-------|-------|------|
| 0 | 10 | 0.00 | 0.00 | 0.00 | 243.44 |
| 10 | 9.9 | 0.00 | 3.61 | 0.00 | 208.81 |
| 30 | 9.7 | 0.00 | 9.36 | 0.34 | 146.23 |
| 50 | 9.5 | 0.00 | 6.95 | 2.55 | 120.68 |
| 80 | 9.2 | 0.00 | 3.32 | 5.88 | 82.35 |

Evidently it does not make sense to buy put options with strike prices below $q^{\alpha}(S(T))$. Looking at the table we can see that when $c$ is small, then we buy options which are cheaper. When $c$ is large, we can afford to spend money on options with higher strike price, which offer better protection. A full picture is obtained when we look not only at VaR, but at the distribution of $X$ in Figure 7.5.

In the formulation of (7.21) we have added constraints that we do not take short positions in puts, and that we do not buy more puts than stocks. Exercising such common sense is often necessary when dealing with VaR. If we allow for arbitrary number of put options, then blind reliance on VaR to assess risk may mislead the investor into using catastrophic hedging strategies. For instance, puts with a high strike price, which are more

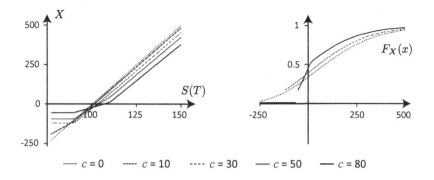

**Figure 7.5** The discounted gain $X_{(x,z)}$ from Example 7.22 for various levels of $c$ (left), and its distribution function (right).

expensive and provide good protection, can be financed by taking short positions in puts whose strike price is below $q^\alpha(S(T))$. Such short positions in puts are ignored in the computation of VaR since their exercise is unlikely. Thus, we can obtain a position with a very small (even negative) VaR.

**Example 7.23**
Consider the data from Example 7.22. Suppose that we want to invest $V_0 = 1000$ and decide to buy $x = 20$ shares of stock and hedge them with $z_2 = 0$ and $z_3 = 20$ put options with strike prices $K_2$ and $K_3$, respectively. Clearly $V(0)$ does not provide enough funds to enter such a position. We decide to finance our strategy by taking a short position in put options with strike price $K_1$

$$z_1 = \frac{1}{H_1(0)}(V_0 - xS(0) - z_3H_3(0)) = -3056.$$

Clearly our strategy is not a good idea. Common sense dictates that the short position in unhedged puts will be catastrophic if $S(T) < K_1$. For instance, if the future price of stock should fall to say 70, then the value of the strategy would be

$$20 \cdot 70 - 3056 \cdot (75 - 70) + 20 \cdot (110 - 70) = -13\,080,$$

leading to a loss exceeding thirteen thousand. Since the probability of this is small,

$$P(S(T) < K_1) < P(S(T) \le q^\alpha(S(T))) = \alpha,$$

such scenarios are ignored in the computation of VaR and we obtain

$$\text{VaR}^\alpha\left(X_{(x,z)}\right) = -1135,$$

indicating a gain of over a thousand at the considered confidence level. This can lull us into a false sense of security, which is visible when comparing VaR with the size of potential losses for $S(T) < K_1$. This once again illustrates the most serious shortcoming of VaR as a risk measure.

We finish the section by showing how to compute VaR for investments in multiple assets. In such case a simple analytic formula for VaR is not available and we make use of the Monte Carlo method discussed in (7.8).

**Example 7.24**

Consider $n$ stocks $S_1, \ldots, S_n$, whose prices at time $T$ evolve according to

$$S_j(T) = S_j(0) \exp\left(\left(\mu_j - \frac{\sigma_j^2}{2}\right)T + \sum_{l=1}^{n} c_{jl}\sqrt{T}Z_l\right),$$

where $Z_1, \ldots, Z_n$ are independent identically distributed random variables (see [PF]) with standard normal distribution $N(0,1)$, $c_{jl} \in \mathbb{R}$ for $j, l = 1, \ldots, n$ are fixed numbers, and

$$\sigma_j = \sqrt{c_{j1}^2 + \cdots + c_{jn}^2}.$$

Such distributions are used in the $n$-dimensional version of the Black–Scholes market (also see [BSM] for details).

Suppose that we split the investment $V(0)$ amongst the securities, buying $x_1, \ldots, x_n$ shares of assets $S_1, \ldots, S_n$, respectively. For $i = 1, \ldots, N$ and $l = 1, \ldots, n$ we can simulate $nN$ independent samples $\hat{Z}_l^i$ from distribution $N(0,1)$, and define

$$\hat{S}_j^i(T) = S_j(0) \exp\left(\left(\mu_j - \frac{\sigma_j^2}{2}\right)T + \sum_{l=1}^{n} c_{jl}\sqrt{T}\hat{Z}_l^i\right).$$

(See [NMFC] for details on how to perform such simulations.) We define

$$\hat{X}_i = e^{-rT} \sum_{j=1}^{n} x_j\hat{S}_j^i(T) - V(0)$$

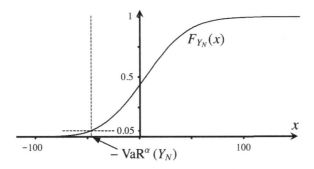

**Figure 7.6** Monte Carlo simulation for VaR in the Black–Scholes market from Example 7.24.

to obtain a sequence of simulated gains that can be used to estimate $\text{VaR}^\alpha(X)$ using (7.8).

In Figure 7.6 we have a plot of $F_{Y_N}$ obtained from $N = 30\,000$ simulations, for the following parameters:

$$S_1(0) = 100, \qquad S_2(0) = 200, \qquad S_3(0) = 300,$$

$$\mu_1 = 10\%, \qquad \mu_2 = 12\%, \qquad \mu_3 = 14\%,$$

$$\begin{bmatrix} c_{11} & c_{12} & c_{13} \\ c_{21} & c_{22} & c_{23} \\ c_{31} & c_{32} & c_{33} \end{bmatrix} = \begin{bmatrix} 0.1 & 0.05 & 0 \\ 0.05 & 0.2 & -0.1 \\ 0 & -0.1 & 0.4 \end{bmatrix},$$

taking $V(0) = 1000$, $r = 5\%$,

$$x_1 = 3, \qquad x_2 = 2, \qquad x_3 = 1,$$

and $T = \frac{1}{12}$. On the plot we also see that $\text{VaR}^\alpha(Y_N) = 47.5$ results from the simulation.

**Exercise 7.8**  Recreate the numerical results from Example 7.24.

## 7.5  Proofs

**Proposition 7.4**
*Let X, Y be random variables.*
   (i) *$X \geq Y$ implies $q^\alpha(X) \geq q^\alpha(Y)$.*
   (ii) *For any $b \in \mathbb{R}$, $q^\alpha(X + b) = q^\alpha(X) + b$.*
   (iii) *For $b > 0$, $q^\alpha(bX) = bq^\alpha(X)$.*
   (iv) *$q^\alpha(-X) = -q_{1-\alpha}(X)$.*

*Proof*   If $X \geq Y$ then

$$F_X(x) = P(X \leq x) \leq P(Y \leq x) = F_Y(x),$$

hence $\alpha < F_X(x)$ implies that $\alpha < F_Y(x)$. This means that

$$\{x : \alpha < F_X(x)\} \subset \{x : \alpha < F_Y(x)\}$$

which gives

$$q^\alpha(X) = \inf\{x : \alpha < F_X(x)\} \geq \inf\{x : \alpha < F_Y(x)\} = q^\alpha(Y).$$

The second property follows since with $Y = X + b$ we have

$$F_Y(x + b) = P(X + b \leq x + b) = F_X(x),$$

so that

$$\begin{aligned}
q^\alpha(X + b) &= \inf\{x + b : \alpha < F_Y(x + b)\} \\
&= \inf\{x : \alpha < F_Y(x + b)\} + b \\
&= \inf\{x : \alpha < F_X(x)\} + b \\
&= q^\alpha(X) + b.
\end{aligned}$$

Since $P(bX \leq x) = P(X \leq x/b)$ we see similarly that

$$F_{bX}(x) = F_X(x/b),$$

hence for $b > 0$

$$\begin{aligned}
q^\alpha(bX) &= \inf\{x : \alpha < F_{bX}(x)\} \\
&= \inf\{x : \alpha < F_X(x/b)\} \\
&= \inf\{by : \alpha < F_X(y)\} \\
&= b\inf\{y : \alpha < F_X(y)\} \\
&= bq^\alpha(X).
\end{aligned}$$

To prove (iv) we first need to show that for any $b \in \mathbb{R}$

$$\inf\{x : b \leq P(X \leq x)\} = \inf\{x : b \leq P(X < x)\}. \tag{7.22}$$

Since $P(X < x) \leq P(X \leq x)$, if $b \leq P(X < x)$ then $b \leq P(X \leq x)$, which means that

$$\{x : b \leq P(X < x)\} \subset \{x : b \leq P(X \leq x)\},$$

hence

$$\inf\{x : b \leq P(X < x)\} \geq \inf\{x : b \leq P(X \leq x)\}.$$

We shall now rule out the possibility that the above inequality is strict. Suppose that

$$\inf\{x : b \leq P(X \leq x)\} < x^* < \inf\{x : b \leq P(X < x)\}, \qquad (7.23)$$

for some $x^* \in \mathbb{R}$. Then $P(X < x^*) < b$, and since $x \to P(X < x)$ is left-continuous, we can find an $\hat{x} \in \mathbb{R}$,

$$\inf\{x : b \leq P(X \leq x)\} < \hat{x} < x^*,$$

for which

$$P(X < \hat{x}) < b. \qquad (7.24)$$

Since $\hat{x}$ is greater than $\inf\{x : b \leq P(X \leq x)\}$, we have

$$b \leq P(X \leq \hat{x}),$$

which contradicts (7.24). We thus must have an equality in (7.23), hence (7.22).

To prove (iv) we shall also use the fact that

$$F_{-X}(x) = P(-X \leq x) = P(X \geq -x) = 1 - P(X < -x). \qquad (7.25)$$

We can now compute

$$
\begin{aligned}
q^\alpha(-X) &= \inf\{x : \alpha < F_{-X}(x)\} \\
&= -\sup\{-x : \alpha < F_{-X}(x)\} \\
&= -\sup\{-x : \alpha < 1 - P(X < -x)\} \\
&\qquad \text{(using (7.25))} \\
&= -\sup\{y : \alpha < 1 - P(X < y)\} \\
&\qquad \text{(taking } y = -x) \\
&= -\sup\{y : P(X < y) < 1 - \alpha\} \\
&= -\inf\{y : 1 - \alpha \le P(X < y)\} \\
&\qquad \text{(since } y \to P(X < y) \text{ is non-decreasing)} \\
&= -\inf\{y : 1 - \alpha \le P(X \le y)\} \\
&\qquad \text{(using (7.22))} \\
&= -\inf\{y : 1 - \alpha \le F_X(y)\} \\
&= -q_{1-\alpha}(X),
\end{aligned}
$$

as required.                                                                  □

### Lemma 7.6

*Let $X$ be a random variable. If $f : \mathbb{R} \to \mathbb{R}$ is right-continuous and non-decreasing then*

$$
q^\alpha(f(X)) = f(q^\alpha(X)).
$$

*Proof*  Since

$$
\begin{aligned}
F_{f(X)}(f(q^\alpha(X))) &= P(f(X) \le f(q^\alpha(X))) \\
&\ge P(X \le q^\alpha(X)) \\
&= F_X(q^\alpha(X)) \\
&\ge \alpha,
\end{aligned}
$$

we see that

$$
f(q^\alpha(X)) \ge q_\alpha(f(X)).
$$

If we can show that $y \ge q^\alpha(f(X))$ whenever $y > f(q^\alpha(X))$, then $f(q^\alpha(X))$ is the largest $\alpha$-quantile for $f(X)$.

Take any $y > f(q^\alpha(X))$. Since $f$ is right-continuous and non-decreasing, the set $f^{-1}(-\infty, y)$ is an open interval of the form $(-\infty, a)$, for some $a \in \mathbb{R}$. This gives

$$
(-\infty, q^\alpha(X)] \subset \{x : f(x) \le f(q^\alpha(X))\} \subset \{x : f(x) < y\} = (-\infty, a),
$$

which means that there exists an $x^*$ for which $q^\alpha(X) < x^* < a$. Since $q^\alpha(X) < x^*$

$$\alpha < F_X(x^*),$$

hence, with $Y = f(X)$,

$$F_Y(y) = P(Y \leq y) \geq P(Y < y) = P(X < a) \geq P(X \leq x^*) = F_X(x^*) > \alpha,$$

which implies that $y \geq q^\alpha(Y) = q^\alpha(f(X))$. $\qquad\qquad\square$

# 8

---

# Coherent measures of risk

---

In the previous chapter Value at Risk was shown to have two potentially undesirable features:

- VaR provides no information on the size of potential losses in scenarios with probability less than $\alpha$.
- VaR recorded for a diversified position may exceed that recorded for a position with all funds held in one security.

On the other hand, VaR has the advantage of simplicity: it produces a single number to quantify the risk of holding a given risky position. However, it does this by taking account only of the $\alpha$-quantile, rather than of the whole distribution.

While VaR has retained much of its popularity with practitioners, many observers have commented that the 2007/8 banking crisis revealed that financial markets can be unduly optimistic in their evaluations of risk. This chapter takes its title from a seminal paper by Artzner, Delbaen, Eber and Heath in 1999,[1] which highlighted the defects of VaR and proceeded to set out, as axioms, four algebraic properties for risk measures to be **coherent**, as well describing a wide class of such measures. This approach has since won many adherents and spawned a very considerable research literature, including further generalisations.

We introduce particular examples of coherent measures, beginning with

---

[1] P. Artzner, F. Delbaen, J.-M. Eber, D. Heath, Coherent measures of risk, *Mathematical Finance* 9, (1999), 203–228.

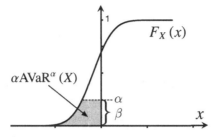

**Figure 8.1** $\alpha$ times AVaR$^\alpha(X)$ is the area for the loss corresponding to the tail of the distribution.

the most natural adaptation of VaR, widely known as AVaR. We will derive equivalent expressions for this risk measure, show that it is sub-additive, compare it with other risk measures proposed as alternatives to VaR, and outline its generalisation to spectral measures. We will also examine AVaR in the Black–Scholes model by revisiting, with AVaR replacing VaR, the hedging techniques with European puts described in Section 7.4.

## 8.1 Average Value at Risk

We first examine how one might modify the definition of VaR to produce a measure of risk that retains simplicity without having the first shortcoming of VaR described above, by taking account of the entire $\alpha$-tail of the distribution. This is mostly simply provided by calculating VaR$^\beta$ for all $\beta \le \alpha$ in $(0, 1)$ and taking their average.

We assume that $X$ denotes the (discounted) gain of some investment project.

**Definition 8.1**
The **Average Value at Risk** of $X$ is given by

$$\text{AVaR}^\alpha(X) = \frac{1}{\alpha} \int_0^\alpha \text{VaR}^\beta(X) d\beta = -\frac{1}{\alpha} \int_0^\alpha q^\beta(X) d\beta.$$

In Figure 8.1 the integral in the definition of AVaR$^\alpha(X)$ is marked as the shaded area for the loss corresponding to the tail of the distribution.

The properties of quantiles given in Proposition 7.4 from the previous chapter show that

$$\text{AVaR}^\alpha(X) = -\frac{1}{\alpha} \int_0^\alpha q^\beta(X) d\beta = \frac{1}{\alpha} \int_0^\alpha q_{1-\beta}(-X) d\beta.$$

Unlike VaR$^\alpha$, this takes into account the impact of all the losses that occur with probability at most $\alpha$: it provides an estimate of the losses implied by events in the $\alpha$-tail of the distribution of X. Informally, AVaR$^\alpha$ provides the 'expected loss, conditioned on the worst $100\alpha$%' of outcomes, whereas VaR$^\alpha$ provides the maximum loss in the 'best $100(1 - \alpha)$%' of outcomes.

Recall that since the distribution function $F_X$ of X is non-decreasing, it can have at most countably many jump discontinuities. This has the advantage that AVaR$^\alpha(X)$ does not depend on the choice of the upper or lower $\alpha$-quantile, unlike the definition of VaR$^\alpha(X)$.

It seems natural to call AVaR the average value-at-risk, although the terms 'conditional value at risk' (CVaR ) or 'expected shortfall' (ES) are also widely used in the literature for quantities that turn out to be equivalent to AVaR.

Since $\beta \le \alpha$ implies $q^\beta(X) \le q^\alpha(X)$ it is clear that AVaR dominates VaR:

$$\text{AVaR}^\alpha(X) = -\frac{1}{\alpha}\int_0^\alpha q^\beta(X)d\beta \ge -\frac{1}{\alpha}\int_0^\alpha q^\alpha(X)d\beta = -q^\alpha(X) = \text{VaR}^\alpha(X).$$

It is immediate from its definition that AVaR will share the properties of VaR we recorded in Proposition 7.9.

**Proposition 8.2**
*For $X \le Y$ and any real number m we have:*
  (i) AVaR$^\alpha(X) \ge$ AVaR$^\alpha(Y)$;
  (ii) AVaR$^\alpha(X + m) =$ AVaR$^\alpha(X) - m$;
  (iii) *for $\lambda \ge 0$,* AVaR$^\alpha(\lambda X) = \lambda$AVaR$^\alpha(X)$.

---

**Exercise 8.1** Verify properties (i)–(iii) in Proposition 8.2.

---

By its definition, AVaR provides a remedy for the first shortcoming of VaR noted earlier, since it takes into account the whole $\alpha$-tail of the distribution. The second problem we noted was that VaR can suggest increased risk when portfolios are diversified. To show that AVaR does not share this defect we need to show that it is **sub-additive**; in other words, that AVaR has the following property:

**Theorem 8.3 (Sub-additivity of AVaR)**
*For any portfolios X, Y*

$$\text{AVaR}^\alpha(X + Y) \le \text{AVaR}^\alpha(X) + \text{AVaR}^\alpha(Y).$$

This property is not evident directly from our definition of AVaR, and the next section is devoted to proving this claim. The proof is given in Corollary 8.11, which follows from Theorem 8.10.

## 8.2 Quantiles and representations of AVaR

In this section we derive an alternative formulation for AVaR, which will be used for the proof of Theorem 8.3. It will also prove useful for calculations in various examples.

We start with a technical lemma.

**Lemma 8.4**

*Let $X : \Omega \to \mathbb{R}$ be a random variable. Assume that $U$ is a uniformly distributed random variable on $(0, 1)$. Then the random variable $Y$, defined by $Y(x) = q^{U(x)}(X)$, has the same distribution as $X$.*

*Proof*   See page 154.                                                                   □

---

**Exercise 8.2**   Prove that Lemma 8.4 holds also for $Y(\omega) = q_{U(\omega)}(X)$.

---

Now, with $f_U$ denoting the uniform density on $(0, 1)$

$$f_U(x) = \begin{cases} 1 & \text{if } x \in (0, 1), \\ 0 & \text{otherwise,} \end{cases}$$

we have

$$\mathbb{E}(Y) = \int_{\mathbb{R}} q^s(X) f_U(s) ds = \int_0^1 q^s(X) ds.$$

Hence Lemma 8.4 implies that for any integrable random variable $X$ we have

$$\int_0^1 q^s(X) ds = \mathbb{E}(Y) = \mathbb{E}(X), \tag{8.1}$$

since the distributions of $X$ and $Y$ are the same.

---

**Exercise 8.3**   Show that (8.1) holds also when we replace $q^s(X)$ with $q_s(X)$.

We now apply (8.1) to obtain an alternative description of AVaR.

**Proposition 8.5**

*For any $\alpha \in (0, 1)$*

$$\text{AVaR}^\alpha(X) = -\frac{1}{\alpha}\left[\mathbb{E}(X\mathbf{1}_{\{X<q^\alpha(X)\}}) + q^\alpha(X)(\alpha - P(X < q^\alpha(X)))\right]. \qquad (8.2)$$

*Proof* Let $x^-$ denote the negative part of $x$, i.e. $x^- = -\min\{x, 0\}$. Since $f(x) = -x^-$ is a non-decreasing function, by Lemma 7.6 for any random variable $Y$ and any $\beta \in (0, 1)$,

$$q^\beta(-Y^-) = q^\beta(f(Y)) = f(q^\beta(Y)) = -(q^\beta(Y))^-. \qquad (8.3)$$

Let us write $q^\alpha(X) = q^\alpha$ for ease of notation. The claim now follows by computing

$$
\begin{aligned}
\text{AVaR}^\alpha(X) &= -\frac{1}{\alpha}\int_0^\alpha q^\beta(X)d\beta \\
&= -\frac{1}{\alpha}\int_0^\alpha (q^\beta(X) - q^\alpha)d\beta - q^\alpha \\
&= -\frac{1}{\alpha}\int_0^1 -(q^\beta(X) - q^\alpha)^- d\beta - q^\alpha && \text{(for } \beta \le \alpha, \ q^\beta(X) \le q^\alpha) \\
&= -\frac{1}{\alpha}\int_0^1 -(q^\beta(X - q^\alpha))^- d\beta - q^\alpha && \text{(by Proposition 7.4)} \\
&= -\frac{1}{\alpha}\int_0^1 q^\beta(-(X - q^\alpha)^-)d\beta - q^\alpha && \text{(using (8.3))} \\
&= -\frac{1}{\alpha}\mathbb{E}(-(X - q^\alpha)^-) - q^\alpha && \text{(using (8.1))} \\
&= -\frac{1}{\alpha}\int_{\{X<q^\alpha\}}(X - q^\alpha)dP - q^\alpha \\
&= -\frac{1}{\alpha}\left[\int_{\{X<q^\alpha\}} XdP - \int_{\{X<q^\alpha\}} q^\alpha dP + \alpha q^\alpha\right] \\
&= -\frac{1}{\alpha}\left[\mathbb{E}(X\mathbf{1}_{\{X<q^\alpha\}}) + q^\alpha(\alpha - P(X < q^\alpha))\right].
\end{aligned}
$$

$\square$

We can now formulate a corollary that allows us to compute AVaR for discretely distributed random variables.

**Corollary 8.6**
*Assume that $X$ is a discrete random variable with $P(X = x_i) = p_i$, $p_1 + \cdots + p_N = 1$, and $x_1 < x_2 < \cdots < x_N$. Then*

$$\text{AVaR}^\alpha(X) = -\frac{1}{\alpha}\left[\sum_{i=1}^{k_\alpha-1} p_i x_i + x_{k_\alpha}\left(\alpha - \sum_{i=1}^{k_\alpha-1} p_i\right)\right],$$

*where $k_\alpha \in \mathbb{N}$ is the largest number such that $\sum_{i=1}^{k_\alpha-1} p_i \le \alpha$.*

*Proof* By Lemma 7.13, $q^\alpha(X) = -\text{VaR}^\alpha(X) = x_{k_\alpha}$, hence

$$P(X < q^\alpha(X)) = \sum_{i=1}^{k_\alpha-1} p_i,$$

$$\mathbb{E}(X\mathbf{1}_{\{X<q^\alpha(X)\}}) = \sum_{i=1}^{k_\alpha-1} p_i x_i,$$

and the claim follows from Proposition 8.5. □

Similarly as for VaR, Corollary 8.6 can be used to estimate AVaR using a Monte Carlo simulation. If $\hat{X}_1, \ldots, \hat{X}_N$ are results of simulations following the same distribution as $X$, we define $Y_N$ as the discrete random variable with distribution

$$P(Y_N = \hat{X}_i) = \frac{1}{N} \qquad \text{for } i = 1, \ldots, N.$$

Since the distribution function $F_{Y_N}$ converges to $F_X$ as $N$ tends to infinity, for sufficiently large $N$ we can approximate $\text{AVaR}^\alpha(X)$ by $\text{AVaR}^\alpha(Y_N)$,

$$\text{AVaR}^\alpha(X) \approx \text{AVaR}^\alpha(Y_N). \tag{8.4}$$

Each $\text{AVaR}^\alpha(Y_N)$ can easily be computed using Corollary 8.6. We shall implement this method in the following section, to compute AVaR in the $n$-dimensional Black–Scholes market (see Example 8.21).

From Proposition 8.5 we also have the following:

**Corollary 8.7**
*If $X$ is a random variable whose distribution function $F_X$ is strictly increasing and continuous, then*

$$\text{AVaR}^\alpha(X) = -\mathbb{E}(X|X \le q^\alpha(X)).$$

*Proof* See page 155. □

For general distributions we need to allow for the possibility that $F_X$ has a jump at $\alpha$. The following lemma is helpful here.

**Lemma 8.8**

*For $\alpha \in (0, 1)$, let $q^\alpha = q^\alpha(X)$ and set*

$$1_X^\alpha - \begin{cases} \mathbf{1}_{\{X < q^\alpha\}} & \text{if } P(X = q^\alpha) = 0, \\ \mathbf{1}_{\{X < q^\alpha\}} + \kappa \mathbf{1}_{\{X = q^\alpha\}} & \text{if } P(X = q^\alpha) > 0, \end{cases} \tag{8.5}$$

*where*

$$\kappa = \frac{\alpha - P(X < q^\alpha)}{P(X = q^\alpha)}. \tag{8.6}$$

*Then*

$$\mathbb{E}(1_X^\alpha) = \alpha, \tag{8.7}$$

*and for all $\omega \in \Omega$,*

$$1_X^\alpha(\omega) \in [0, 1]. \tag{8.8}$$

*Proof* See page 156. □

The reason for the definition of $\mathbf{1}_X^\alpha$ becomes clear in the next proposition, which allows us to express AVaR$^\alpha$ as an expectation.

**Proposition 8.9**

*For any $\alpha \in (0, 1)$,*

$$\text{AVaR}^\alpha(X) = -\frac{1}{\alpha}\mathbb{E}(X1_X^\alpha).$$

*Proof* As above, write $q^\alpha(X) = q^\alpha$. If $P(X = q^\alpha) = 0$, then $P(X < q^\alpha) = P(X \le q^\alpha) = \alpha$, so that the second term on the right in (8.2) vanishes and

$$\text{AVaR}^\alpha(X) = -\frac{1}{\alpha}\mathbb{E}(X1_{\{X < q^\alpha\}}) = -\frac{1}{\alpha}\mathbb{E}(X1_X^\alpha).$$

If $P(X = q^\alpha) > 0$, then using the fact that

$$\int_{\{X = q^\alpha\}} XdP = \int_{\{X = q^\alpha\}} q^\alpha dP = q^\alpha P(X = q^\alpha), \tag{8.9}$$

we compute

$$\begin{aligned}
\mathbb{E}(X1_X^\alpha) &= \mathbb{E}\left(X1_{\{X < q^\alpha\}} + X\tfrac{\alpha - P(X < q^\alpha)}{P(X = q^\alpha)}1_{\{X = q^\alpha\}}\right) \\
&= \mathbb{E}(X1_{\{X < q^\alpha\}}) + \int_{\{X = q^\alpha\}} X\tfrac{\alpha - P(X < q^\alpha)}{P(X = q^\alpha)}dP \\
&= \mathbb{E}(X1_{\{X < q^\alpha\}}) + \tfrac{\alpha - P(X < q^\alpha)}{P(X = q^\alpha)}\int_{\{X = q^\alpha\}} XdP \\
&= \mathbb{E}(X1_{\{X < q^\alpha\}}) + q^\alpha(\alpha - P(X < q^\alpha)) \quad \text{(using (8.9))} \\
&= -\alpha\text{AVaR}^\alpha(X), \quad\quad\quad\quad\quad\quad\quad\quad \text{(using (8.2))}
\end{aligned}$$

as required. □

Let us observe that the random variable $Z(\omega) = \frac{1}{\alpha}\mathbf{1}_X^\alpha(\omega)$ is integrable, bounded above by $\frac{1}{\alpha}$ and has expectation 1, as shown in Lemma 8.8. We can therefore define a new probability measure, which we denote by $Q_X^\alpha$, as

$$Q_X^\alpha(A) = \int_A Z\, dP.$$

In other words, $Z$ is a Radon–Nikodym derivative, and the usual notation is to write

$$Z = \frac{dQ_X^\alpha}{dP}.$$

(See [PF] for the definition of the Radon–Nikodym derivative and for more details.)

This shows that, using the measure $Q_X^\alpha$, the expression for AVaR$^\alpha$ takes a surprisingly simple form

$$\text{AVaR}^\alpha(X) = -\frac{1}{\alpha}\mathbb{E}\left(X\mathbf{1}_X^\alpha\right) = -\frac{1}{\alpha}\int_\Omega X\mathbf{1}_X^\alpha dP = -\int_\Omega X\frac{dQ_X^\alpha}{dP}dP = -\mathbb{E}_{Q_X^\alpha}(X).$$

This will lead to a simple proof of its sub-additivity. First we need a representation result.

Recall that a probability measure $Q$ is absolutely continuous with respect to $P$, which we denote as $Q \ll P$, when $P(A) = 0$ implies $Q(A) = 0$. By the Radon–Nikodym theorem (see [PF]), for any $Q$ absolutely continuous with respect to $P$ there exists a Radon–Nikodym derivative $\frac{dQ}{dP}$, meaning that

$$Q(A) = \int_A \frac{dQ}{dP}dP.$$

**Theorem 8.10**
*For $\alpha \in (0, 1)$ let*

$$\mathcal{P}_\alpha = \left\{Q : Q \text{ is a probability measure, } Q \ll P, \frac{dQ}{dP} \le \frac{1}{\alpha}\right\}.$$

*Then*

$$\sup\{-\mathbb{E}_Q(X) : Q \in \mathcal{P}_\alpha\} = \text{AVaR}^\alpha(X).$$

*Proof* Let us write $q^\alpha = q^\alpha(X)$. Since

$$\frac{dQ_X^\alpha}{dP}(\omega) = \frac{1}{\alpha}\mathbf{1}_X^\alpha(\omega),$$

looking at the definition of $\mathbf{1}_X^\alpha$ in (8.5), we see that

$$\frac{dQ_X^\alpha}{dP}(\omega) = \frac{1}{\alpha} \qquad \text{for } \omega \in \{X < q^\alpha\}, \tag{8.10}$$

$$\frac{dQ_X^\alpha}{dP}(\omega) = \frac{1}{\alpha}\kappa \qquad \text{for } \omega \in \{X = q^\alpha\}, \tag{8.11}$$

$$\frac{dQ_X^\alpha}{dP}(\omega) = 0 \qquad \text{for } \omega \in \{X > q^\alpha\}. \tag{8.12}$$

Let $Q$ be an arbitrary measure in $\mathcal{P}_\alpha$. We compute

$$
\begin{aligned}
\mathbb{E}_Q(X) &= \int_\Omega X \frac{dQ}{dP} dP \\
&= \int_{\{X<q^\alpha\}} X \frac{dQ}{dP} dP + \int_{\{X=q^\alpha\}} X \frac{dQ}{dP} dP + \int_{\{X>q^\alpha\}} X \frac{dQ}{dP} dP \\
&= \int_{\{X<q^\alpha\}} X \left(\frac{dQ}{dP} - \frac{1}{\alpha}\right) dP + \int_{\{X<q^\alpha\}} X \frac{dQ_X^\alpha}{dP} dP \qquad \text{(see (8.10))} \\
&\quad + \int_{\{X=q^\alpha\}} X \left(\frac{dQ}{dP} - \frac{1}{\alpha}\kappa\right) dP + \int_{\{X=q^\alpha\}} X \frac{dQ_X^\alpha}{dP} dP \qquad \text{(see (8.11))} \\
&\quad + \int_{\{X>q^\alpha\}} X \frac{dQ}{dP} dP + \int_{\{X>q^\alpha\}} X \frac{dQ_X^\alpha}{dP} dP \qquad \text{(see (8.12))} \\
&= \int_{\{X<q^\alpha\}} X \left(\frac{dQ}{dP} - \frac{1}{\alpha}\right) dP + \int_{\{X=q^\alpha\}} X \left(\frac{dQ}{dP} - \frac{1}{\alpha}\kappa\right) dP \\
&\quad + \int_{\{X>q^\alpha\}} X \frac{dQ}{dP} dP + \int_\Omega X \frac{dQ_X^\alpha}{dP} dP.
\end{aligned}
$$

We now examine one by one the four integrals in the above expression. By definition, $\frac{dQ}{dP} \leq \frac{1}{\alpha}$, hence on $\{X < q^\alpha\}$

$$(X - q^\alpha)\left(\frac{dQ}{dP} - \frac{1}{\alpha}\right) \geq 0,$$

giving

$$\int_{\{X<q^\alpha\}} X \left(\frac{dQ}{dP} - \frac{1}{\alpha}\right) dP \geq \int_{\{X<q^\alpha\}} q^\alpha \left(\frac{dQ}{dP} - \frac{1}{\alpha}\right) dP. \tag{8.13}$$

Evidently,

$$\int_{\{X=q^\alpha\}} X \left(\frac{dQ}{dP} - \frac{1}{\alpha}\kappa\right) dP = \int_{\{X=q^\alpha\}} q^\alpha \left(\frac{dQ}{dP} - \frac{1}{\alpha}\kappa\right) dP. \tag{8.14}$$

Since $\frac{dQ}{dP} \geq 0$,

$$\int_{\{X>q^\alpha\}} X \frac{dQ}{dP} dP \geq \int_{\{X>q^\alpha\}} q^\alpha \frac{dQ}{dP} dP. \tag{8.15}$$

Finally, for the last of the four integrals we see that

$$\int_\Omega X \frac{dQ_X^\alpha}{dP} dP = \mathbb{E}_{Q_X^\alpha}(X). \tag{8.16}$$

Substituting (8.13)–(8.16) into our formula for $\mathbb{E}_Q(X)$ we obtain

$$
\mathbb{E}_Q(X) \geq \int_{\{X<q^\alpha\}} q^\alpha \left(\frac{dQ}{dP} - \frac{1}{\alpha}\right) dP + \int_{\{X=q^\alpha\}} q^\alpha \left(\frac{dQ}{dP} - \frac{1}{\alpha}\kappa\right) dP
$$
$$
+ \int_{\{X>q^\alpha\}} q^\alpha \frac{dQ}{dP} dP + \mathbb{E}_{Q_X^\alpha}(X)
$$
$$
= -\int_{\{X<q^\alpha\}} q^\alpha \frac{1}{\alpha} dP - \int_{\{X=q^\alpha\}} q^\alpha \frac{1}{\alpha}\kappa dP
$$
$$
+ \int_\Omega q^\alpha \frac{dQ}{dP} dP + \mathbb{E}_{Q_X^\alpha}(X)
$$
$$
= -q^\alpha \frac{1}{\alpha} P(X < q^\alpha) - q^\alpha \frac{1}{\alpha}\kappa P(X = q^\alpha) + q^\alpha + \mathbb{E}_{Q_X^\alpha}(X)
$$
$$
= \mathbb{E}_{Q_X^\alpha}(X). \qquad \text{(using (8.6))}
$$

We have shown that $-\mathbb{E}_Q(X) \leq -\mathbb{E}_{Q_\alpha}(X)$. Since $Q_X^\alpha \in \mathcal{P}_\alpha$, this implies that

$$
\sup\{-\mathbb{E}_Q(X) : Q \in \mathcal{P}_\alpha\} = -\mathbb{E}_{Q_X^\alpha}(X) = \text{AVaR}^\alpha(X),
$$

as required. □

We are finally ready to prove Theorem 8.3. The result follows from Theorem 8.10 and we formulate it as a corollary.

**Corollary 8.11**
AVaR *is sub-additive:*

$$
\text{AVaR}^\alpha(X + Y) \leq \text{AVaR}^\alpha(X) + \text{AVaR}^\alpha(Y).
$$

*Proof* We use the fact that for two functions $f, g : U \to \mathbb{R}$, where $U$ is an arbitrary set,

$$
\sup_{x\in U}\{f(x) + g(x)\} \leq \sup_{x\in U} f(x) + \sup_{x\in U} g(x). \tag{8.17}
$$

Let us fix $X$ and $Y$. We can apply (8.17) taking $U = \mathcal{P}_\alpha$, $f(Q) = -\mathbb{E}_Q(X)$, and $g(Q) = -\mathbb{E}_Q(Y)$ to obtain

$$
\begin{aligned}
\text{AVaR}^\alpha(X + Y) &= \sup\{-\mathbb{E}_Q(X + Y) : Q \in \mathcal{P}_\alpha\} \\
&= \sup\{\mathbb{E}_Q(-X) + \mathbb{E}_Q(-Y) : Q \in \mathcal{P}_\alpha\} \\
&\leq \sup\{\mathbb{E}_Q(-X) : Q \in \mathcal{P}_\alpha\} + \sup\{\mathbb{E}_Q(-Y) : Q \in \mathcal{P}_\alpha\} \\
&\qquad \text{(using (8.17))} \\
&= \text{AVaR}^\alpha(X) + \text{AVaR}^\alpha(Y),
\end{aligned}
$$

as required. □

The next exercise provides an alternative direct proof of sub-additivity. The idea is the same as in the proof of Theorem 8.10.

---

**Exercise 8.4**    Let AVaR be defined by (8.2). Given a probability space $(\Omega, \mathcal{F}, P)$ and random variables $X, Y : \Omega \to \mathbb{R}$ with $Z = X + Y$, show that

$$1_Z^\alpha - 1_X^\alpha \geq 0 \text{ if } X > q_\alpha(X)$$
$$1_Z^\alpha - 1_X^\alpha \leq 0 \text{ if } X < q_\alpha(X)$$

and similarly with $X$ replaced by $Y$. Exploit this fact to show that AVaR is sub-additive: $\text{AVaR}^\alpha(Z) \leq \text{AVaR}^\alpha(X) + \text{AVaR}^\alpha(Y)$.

---

We now consider a further risk measure whose definition is similar to the description of AVaR we found in Proposition 8.9.

**Definition 8.12**

We define the (upper) **tail conditional expectation (TCE)** of $X$ as

$$\text{TCE}^\alpha(X) = -\mathbb{E}(X|X \leq q^\alpha(X)) = -\mathbb{E}(X|X \leq -\text{VaR}^\alpha(X)). \qquad (8.18)$$

The next exercise shows that TCE shares the three properties already verified for VaR and AVaR.

---

**Exercise 8.5**    Show that for $X \leq Y$ and any real number $m$ we have:
  (i)  $\text{TCE}^\alpha(X) \geq \text{TCE}^\alpha(Y)$;
  (ii)  $\text{TCE}^\alpha(X + m) = \text{TCE}^\alpha(X) - m$;
  (iii)  for $\lambda \geq 0$, $\text{TCE}^\alpha(\lambda X) = \lambda \text{TCE}^\alpha(X)$.

---

When $F_X$ is continuous then $\alpha = P(X \leq q^\alpha(X)) = P(X < q^\alpha(X))$. Hence for continuous $F_X$ we have

$$\text{TCE}^\alpha(X) = \text{AVaR}^\alpha(X). \qquad (8.19)$$

Comparing (8.2) with (8.18) we see that $\text{TCE}^\alpha$ has a simpler expression than $\text{AVaR}^\alpha$. A natural question is therefore whether TCE is sub-additive in general. The next example shows that this is not true.

**Example 8.13**

Let $\Omega = \{\omega_1, \omega_2, \omega_3\}$ and

$$P(\{\omega_1\}) = P(\{\omega_2\}) = 0.03,$$
$$P(\{\omega_3\}) = 0.94.$$

Let $\alpha = 0.05$ and define random variables $X, Y$ by setting

$$X(\omega_1) = -100, \qquad X(\omega_2) = 0, \qquad X(\omega_3) = 0,$$
$$Y(\omega_1) = 0, \qquad Y(\omega_2) = -100, \qquad Y(\omega_3) = 0.$$

We claim that

$$\mathrm{TCE}^\alpha(X + Y) > \mathrm{TCE}^\alpha(X) + \mathrm{TCE}^\alpha(Y).$$

Since

$$q^\alpha(X) = \inf\{x : F_X(x) > 0.05\} = 0,$$

and $\{X \leq 0\} = \Omega$, we see that

$$\mathrm{TCE}^\alpha(X) = -\mathbb{E}\left(X | X \leq q^\alpha(X)\right) = -\mathbb{E}\left(X | \Omega\right) = -\mathbb{E}(X)$$
$$= -[0.03 \times (-100) + 0.97 \times 0] = 3.$$

By an identical computation, also

$$\mathrm{TCE}^\alpha(Y) = 3.$$

On the other hand, $Z = X + Y$ has

$$q^\alpha(Z) = \inf\{x : F_Z(x) > 0.05\} = -100,$$

and $\{Z \leq q^\alpha(Z)\} = \{\omega_1, \omega_2\}$, hence

$$\mathrm{TCE}^\alpha(Z) = -\mathbb{E}(Z | Z \leq q^\alpha(Z))$$
$$= -\frac{1}{P(Z \leq q^\alpha(Z))}\left(Z(\omega_1)P(\{\omega_1\}) + Z(\omega_1)P(\{\omega_1\})\right)$$
$$= -\frac{1}{0.06}(-100 \times 0.03 - 100 \times 0.03)$$
$$= 100.$$

This demonstrates a serious shortcoming of the tail-conditional expectation as a risk measure. Since

$$\mathrm{TCE}^\alpha\left(\frac{1}{2}X + \frac{1}{2}Y\right) = \frac{1}{2}\mathrm{TCE}^\alpha(X + Y) \geq \frac{1}{2}\left[\mathrm{TCE}^\alpha(X) + \mathrm{TCE}^\alpha(Y)\right],$$

the diversified position consisting of investing one-half of our funds in each of $X$ and $Y$ is riskier than placing the whole fund in one or the other.

The example shows that TCE shares the same defect as VaR. Fortunately AVaR, even though its computation is slightly more involved, has much more desirable properties.

**Exercise 8.6**   Consider the same $X$ and $Y$ as in Example 8.13. Compute $\text{AVaR}^\alpha(X)$, $\text{AVaR}^\alpha(Y)$ and $\text{AVaR}^\alpha(X + Y)$, and compare with the above Example.

## 8.3   AVaR in the Black–Scholes model

In this section we discuss how to compute AVaR in the setting of the Black–Scholes model. Let us recall that, under the assumptions of the model, the future stock price at time $T$ is

$$S(T) = S(0)e^{\left(\left(\mu - \frac{\sigma^2}{2}\right)T + \sigma\sqrt{T}Z\right)}, \tag{8.20}$$

where $S(0), \mu \in \mathbb{R}$, $\sigma > 0$, and $Z$ is a random variable with standard normal distribution $N(0, 1)$.

Before computing AVaR, we start with a technical lemma.

**Lemma 8.14**
*For any $q \in \mathbb{R}$*

$$\mathbb{E}\left(S(T)|Z \le q\right) = \frac{1}{N(q)}S(0)e^{\mu T}N\left(q - \sigma\sqrt{T}\right),$$

*where $N(q)$ is the standard normal cumulative distribution function, i.e.*

$$N(q) = \int_{-\infty}^{q} \frac{1}{\sqrt{2\pi}}e^{-\frac{x^2}{2}}dx.$$

*Proof* Since $P(Z \le q) = N(q) > 0$,

$$\mathbb{E}\,(S(T)|Z \le q) = \frac{1}{P(Z \le q)} \int_{-\infty}^{q} S(0)e^{\left(\left(\mu - \frac{\sigma^2}{2}\right)T + \sigma\sqrt{T}x\right)} \frac{1}{\sqrt{2\pi}} e^{-\frac{x^2}{2}} dx$$

$$= \frac{1}{N(q)} S(0)e^{\left(\mu - \frac{\sigma^2}{2}\right)T} \int_{-\infty}^{q} \frac{1}{\sqrt{2\pi}} e^{-\frac{x^2 - 2\sigma\sqrt{T}x}{2}} dx$$

$$= \frac{1}{N(q)} S(0)e^{\left(\mu - \frac{\sigma^2}{2}\right)T} \int_{-\infty}^{q} \frac{1}{\sqrt{2\pi}} e^{-\frac{x^2 - 2\sigma\sqrt{T}x + \sigma^2 T}{2} + \frac{\sigma^2 T}{2}} dx$$

$$= \frac{1}{N(q)} S(0)e^{\mu T} \int_{-\infty}^{q} \frac{1}{\sqrt{2\pi}} e^{-\frac{\left(x - \sigma\sqrt{T}\right)^2}{2}} dx$$

$$= \frac{1}{N(q)} S(0)e^{\mu T} \int_{-\infty}^{q - \sigma\sqrt{T}} \frac{1}{\sqrt{2\pi}} e^{-\frac{x^2}{2}} dx$$

$$= \frac{1}{N(q)} S(0)e^{\mu T} N\left(q - \sigma\sqrt{T}\right),$$

as required. □

We are now ready to compute AVaR for an investment in stock.

**Lemma 8.15**
*For the discounted gain*

$$X = e^{-rT} S(T) - S(0)$$

*we have*

$$\mathrm{AVaR}^{\alpha}(X) = S(0) - \frac{1}{\alpha} S(0)e^{(\mu - r)T} N\left(q^{\alpha}(Z) - \sigma\sqrt{T}\right).$$

*Proof* By Lemma 7.17 we know that

$$q^{\alpha}(S(T)) = S(0)e^{\left(\left(\mu - \frac{\sigma^2}{2}\right)T + \sigma\sqrt{T}q^{\alpha}(Z)\right)}, \tag{8.21}$$

therefore

$$\{X \le q^{\alpha}(X)\} = \{e^{-rT}S(T) - S(0) \le q^{\alpha}(e^{-rT}S(T) - S(0))\}$$

$$= \{e^{-rT}S(T) - S(0) \le e^{-rT}q^{\alpha}(S(T)) - S(0)\}$$

$$\text{(by Proposition 7.4)}$$

$$= \{S(T) \le q^{\alpha}(S(T))\}$$

$$= \{Z \le q^{\alpha}(Z)\}. \quad \text{(compare (8.20) with (8.21))}$$

Since $X$ has continuous distribution, this gives

$$
\begin{aligned}
\mathrm{AVaR}^\alpha(X) &= \mathrm{TCE}^\alpha(X) \\
&= -\mathbb{E}\left(X | X \le q^\alpha(X)\right) \\
&= -\mathbb{E}\left(e^{-rT}S(T) - S(0) | Z \le q^\alpha(Z)\right) \\
&= S(0) - e^{-rT}\mathbb{E}\left(S(T) | Z \le q^\alpha(Z)\right) \\
&= S(0) - \frac{1}{\alpha}S(0)e^{(\mu-r)T}N\left(q^\alpha(Z) - \sigma\sqrt{T}\right), \quad \text{(by Lemma 8.14)}
\end{aligned}
$$

as required.                                                                 □

---

**Exercise 8.7**  Consider holding $x > 0$ shares of stock $S$ and investing a cash sum $y$ risk-free at time 0. The values of this trading strategy $(x, y)$ at times $0, T$ are

$$
\begin{aligned}
V_{(x,y)}(0) &= xS(0) + y, \\
V_{(x,y)}(T) &= xS(T) + ye^{rT}.
\end{aligned}
$$

Compute $\mathrm{AVaR}^\alpha(X_{(x,y)})$ for

$$
X_{(x,y)} = e^{-rT}V_{(x,y)}(T) - V_{(x,y)}(0).
$$

Show that if $y > 0$, then $\mathrm{AVaR}^\alpha(X_{(x,y)})$ is smaller than AVaR of a position where $V_{(x,y)}(0)$ would be invested only in stock.

---

**Exercise 8.8**  Consider buying $x > 0$ shares of stock $S$ and taking a long position in $\theta \in [0, x]$ forward contracts to sell the stock at time $T$, for the forward price $F = S(0)e^{rT}$. The value of the trading strategy $(x, y)$ is

$$
\begin{aligned}
V_{(x,\theta)}(0) &= S(0), \\
V_{(x,\theta)}(T) &= S(T) + \theta(F - S(T)).
\end{aligned}
$$

Compute $\mathrm{AVaR}^\alpha(X_{(x,\theta)})$ for

$$
X_{(x,\theta)} = e^{-rT}V_{(x,\theta)}(T) - V_{(x,\theta)}(0).
$$

Show that $\mathrm{AVaR}^\alpha(X_{(x,\theta)})$ is smaller than AVaR of a position without the forward contract.

We now turn our attention to hedging AVaR with European put options. Assume that at time zero we buy $x$ shares of stock and $z$ European put options with strike price $K$ and exercise date $T$. The value of the investment is given at $t = 0, T$ by

$$V_{(x,z)}(t) = xS(t) + zH(t),$$

where $H(T)$ is the put option payoff

$$H(T) = (K - S(T))^+,$$

and $H(0)$ is the put option price

$$H(0) = P(r, T, K, S(0), \sigma) = Ke^{-rT}N(-d_-) - S(0)N(-d_+), \qquad (8.22)$$

where

$$d_+ = d_+(r, T, K, S(0), \sigma) = \frac{\ln \frac{S(0)}{K} + \left(r + \frac{1}{2}\sigma^2\right)T}{\sigma \sqrt{T}},$$

$$d_- = d_-(r, T, K, S(0), \sigma) = \frac{\ln \frac{S(0)}{K} + \left(r - \frac{1}{2}\sigma^2\right)T}{\sigma \sqrt{T}}.$$

The discounted gain of the investment is

$$X_{(x,z)} = e^{-rT}V_{(x,z)}(T) - V_{(x,z)}(0).$$

Our aim will be to compute $\text{AVaR}^\alpha(X_{(x,z)})$. First we need to introduce some notation. We write

$$d_-^\mu = d_-(\mu, T, K, S(0), \sigma), \qquad d_+^\mu = d_-^\mu + \sigma \sqrt{T},$$
$$d_-^{\mu,\alpha} = \max\left(d_-^\mu, -q^\alpha(Z)\right), \qquad d_+^{\mu,\alpha} = d_-^{\mu,\alpha} + \sigma \sqrt{T},$$

and

$$P^\alpha(K) = Ke^{-\mu T}N(-d_-^{\mu,\alpha}) - S(0)N(-d_+^{\mu,\alpha}). \qquad (8.23)$$

**Proposition 8.16**
*If $z \in [0, x]$, then*

$$\text{AVaR}^\alpha(X_{(x,z)}) = V_{(x,z)}(0) - \frac{1}{\alpha}e^{(\mu-r)T}\left[xS(0)N\left(q^\alpha(Z) - \sigma\sqrt{T}\right) + zP^\alpha(K)\right].$$

*Proof* We first observe that

$$X_{(x,z)} = e^{-rT}V_{(x,z)}(T) - V_{(x,z)}(0)$$
$$= e^{-rT}\left(xS(T) + z(K - S(T))^+\right) - V_{(x,z)}(0). \qquad (8.24)$$

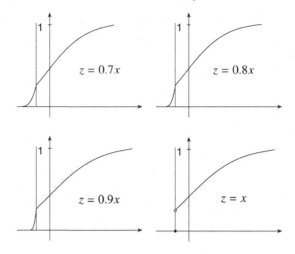

**Figure 8.2** $F_{X_{(x,z)}}$ for various $z$. The dotted line represents $X_{(x,z)}$ for $S(T) = K$.

Since $z \leq x$, we see that

$$s \rightarrow e^{-rT} \left( xs + z(K - s)^+ \right) - V_{(x,z)}(0) \tag{8.25}$$

is a non-decreasing function of $s$. Also

$$\xi \rightarrow S(0) \exp\left( \left( \mu - \frac{\sigma^2}{2} \right) T + \sigma \sqrt{T} \xi \right)$$

is increasing. Combining these two facts, by Lemma 7.6,

$$\{X_{(x,z)} \leq q^\alpha(X_{(x,z)})\} = \{S(T) \leq q^\alpha(S(T))\} = \{Z \leq q^\alpha(Z)\}. \tag{8.26}$$

We first prove the claim for $z < x$. Then (8.25) is strictly increasing, therefore

$$P(X_{(x,y)} < q^\alpha(X_{(x,y)})) = P(S(T) \leq q^\alpha(S(T))) = \alpha,$$

and by Proposition 8.5,

$$\begin{aligned}
\text{AVaR}^\alpha(X_{(x,z)}) &= -\mathbb{E}\left( X_{(x,z)} | X_{(x,z)} \leq q^\alpha(X) \right) \\
&= -\mathbb{E}\left( X_{(x,z)} | Z \leq q^\alpha(Z) \right) && \text{(by (8.26))} \\
&= V_{(x,z)}(0) - e^{-rT} x \mathbb{E}\left( S(T) | Z \leq q^\alpha(Z) \right) && \text{(see (8.24))} \\
&\quad - e^{-rT} z \mathbb{E}\left( (K - S(T))^+ | Z \leq q^\alpha(Z) \right). \tag{8.27}
\end{aligned}$$

We now compute the last term in (8.27). By (8.20),

$$\{S(T) \leq K\} = \{Z \leq -d_-^\mu\},$$

hence,

$$\mathbb{E}\left((K - S(T))^+ \mid Z \le q^\alpha(Z)\right)$$

$$= \mathbb{E}\left((K - S(T))\mathbf{1}_{\{Z \le -d_-^\mu\}} \mid Z \le q^\alpha(Z)\right)$$

$$= \frac{1}{\alpha} \int_{-\infty}^{\min(q^\alpha(Z), -d_-^\mu)} \left(K - S(0)e^{\left(\mu - \frac{\sigma^2}{2}\right)T + \sigma\sqrt{T}x}\right) \frac{1}{\sqrt{2\pi}} e^{-x^2} dx$$

$$= \frac{1}{\alpha} \int_{-\infty}^{-d_-^{\mu,\alpha}} K \frac{1}{\sqrt{2\pi}} e^{-x^2} dx \qquad (\min(a, b) = -\max(-a, -b))$$

$$\quad - \frac{1}{\alpha} \int_{-\infty}^{-d_-^{\mu,\alpha}} S(0)e^{\left(\mu - \frac{\sigma^2}{2}\right)T + \sigma\sqrt{T}x} \frac{1}{\sqrt{2\pi}} e^{-x^2} dx$$

$$= \frac{1}{\alpha} KN(-d_-^{\mu,\alpha}) - \frac{1}{\alpha} P(Z \le -d_-^{\mu,\alpha})\mathbb{E}\left(S(T) \mid Z \le -d_-^{\mu,\alpha}\right)$$

$$= \frac{1}{\alpha} KN(-d_-^{\mu,\alpha}) - \frac{1}{\alpha} S(0)e^{\mu T} N\left(-d_-^{\mu,\alpha} - \sigma\sqrt{T}\right) \qquad \text{(by Lemma 8.14)}$$

$$= \frac{1}{\alpha} e^{\mu T}\left(Ke^{-\mu T} N(-d_-^{\mu,\alpha}) - S(0)N\left(-d_+^{\mu,\alpha}\right)\right).$$

Substituting the above into (8.27) and applying Lemma 8.14 gives the claim.

We now need to consider the case when $z = x$. Since for any $\beta \in (0, 1)$ (see Figure 8.2)

$$\lim_{z \nearrow x} q^\beta(X_{(x,z)}) = q^\beta(X_{(x,x)}),$$

we obtain

$$\lim_{z \nearrow x} \text{AVaR}^\alpha\left(X_{(x,z)}\right) = \lim_{z \nearrow x} \frac{-1}{\alpha} \int_0^\alpha q^\beta(X_{(x,z)}) d\beta$$

$$= \frac{-1}{\alpha} \int_0^\alpha q^\beta(X_{(x,x)}) d\beta$$

$$= \text{AVaR}^\alpha\left(X_{(x,x)}\right).$$

Hence the result follows from the fact that the formula for $\text{AVaR}^\alpha(X_{(x,z)})$ in the claim is continuous with respect to $z$. $\qquad\square$

---

**Exercise 8.9** Show that if $x = z$ and $K \ge q^\alpha(S(T))$, then

$$\text{AVaR}^\alpha(X_{(x,z)}) = \text{VaR}^\alpha(X_{(x,z)}).$$

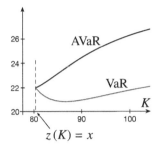

**Figure 8.3** AVaR of a fixed position in $x$ stocks, hedged with puts (parameters of the model are as in Exercise 8.11).

**Example 8.17**
Suppose that we spend $V_0$ to buy a fixed number $x$ of stocks, together with $z$ put options. The number of options we can buy depends on the choice of the strike price $K$,

$$z = z(K) = \frac{V_0 - xS(0)}{P(r, T, K, S(0), \sigma)}.$$

We consider $\text{AVaR}^\alpha(X_{(x,z(K))})$ for $K$ such that $z(K) \leq x$.

In Figure 8.3 we see that the smallest AVaR is attained for the smallest considered strike price, for which $z(K) = x$. On the plot we also see that AVaR dominates VaR, and that the two are equal when $z(K) = x$.

---

**Exercise 8.10**   Show that

$$\mathbb{E}(X_{(x,z)}) = e^{(\mu-r)T} \left[ xS(0) + zP(\mu, T, K, S(0), \sigma) \right] - V_{(x,z)}(0).$$

---

**Example 8.18**
From Example 8.17 we see that AVaR is minimised when we buy the same number of shares of stock and European put options. Suppose therefore that we invest $V_0$ to buy $x$ shares of stock and $x$ puts. Here $x$ depends on the choice of the strike price $K$ (since the higher the strike, the more expensive

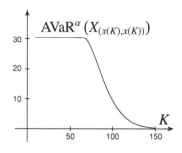 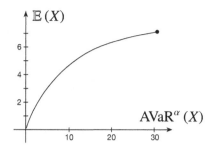

**Figure 8.4** AVaR of a position in the same number of stocks and puts, for data from Exercise 8.11.

the put), and follows from the constraint

$$xS(0) + xP(r, T, K, S(0), \sigma) = V_0,$$

which gives

$$x = x(K) = \frac{V_0}{S(0) + P(r, T, K, S(0), \sigma)}.$$

By making plots of

$$\{(K, \text{AVaR}^\alpha (X_{(x(K), x(K))})) \,|\, K \geq 0\}$$

and

$$\{(\text{AVaR}^\alpha (X_{(x(K), x(K))}), \mathbb{E}(X_{(x(K), x(K))})) \,|\, K \geq 0\},$$

we obtain the graphs shown in Figure 8.4.

On the left-hand plot we can see that a high strike price reduces the AVaR to zero. From the right-hand plot we see, however, that this is done at the expense of also reducing the discounted expected gain to zero.

For $K = 0$ the associated AVaR and expected gain is the same as the one for an investment in stock (represented by the dot in the right-hand plot).

**Exercise 8.11**  Consider $V_0 = 100$, $S(0) = 100$, $\mu = 10\%$, $r = 3\%$ and $\alpha = 0.05$. As in Example 8.18, assume that we buy the same number of shares of stock and European put options. Recreate numerically the plot from Figure 8.4.

Add to the right-hand plot in Figure 8.4 the set of points

$$\left\{\left(\text{AVaR}^\alpha(X_{(x,y)}), \mathbb{E}(X_{(x,y)})\right) \mid y \geq 0, xS(0) + y = V_0\right\},$$

attainable by investing in stock and the risk-free asset.

What is more efficient, hedging AVaR with puts or diversifying between the stock and the risk-free asset?

---

**Exercise 8.12** In a similar fashion to Exercise 8.11, compare hedging with puts and hedging with forward contracts.

---

We now consider what happens when we do not have full freedom of choice of the strike price. Assume that we can invest in $n$ European put options with maturity $T$ and strike prices $K_1, \ldots, K_n$. We denote the value at time $t$ of the option with strike price $K_i$ as $H_i(t)$ and write

$$\mathbf{H}(t) = (H_1(t), \ldots, H_n(t)).$$

Assume that we buy $x$ shares of stock and $z_i$ puts with strike prices $K_i$, for $i = 1, \ldots, n$. The position in puts is determined by the vector

$$\mathbf{z} = (z_1, \ldots, z_n) \in \mathbb{R}^n.$$

The value of our investment at time $t$ is

$$V_{(x,\mathbf{z})}(t) = xS(t) + \mathbf{z}^\mathrm{T}\mathbf{H}(t),$$

and the discounted gain is

$$X_{(x,\mathbf{z})} = e^{-rT}V_{(x,\mathbf{z})}(T) - V_{(x,\mathbf{z})}(0).$$

**Proposition 8.19**
*If $z_i \geq 0$ for $i = 1, \ldots, n$ and $z_1 + \cdots + z_n \leq x$, then*

$$\text{AVaR}^\alpha(X_{(x,\mathbf{z})}) = V_{(x,\mathbf{z})}(0) - \frac{1}{\alpha}e^{(\mu-r)T}\left[xS(0)N\left(q^\alpha(Z) - \sigma\sqrt{T}\right) + \mathbf{z}^\mathrm{T}\mathbf{P}^\alpha\right],$$
(8.28)

*where $\mathbf{P}^\alpha = (P^\alpha(K_1), \ldots, P^\alpha(K_n))$.*

The proof of the proposition follows along the same line as the proof of Proposition 8.16. We leave it as an exercise.

> **Exercise 8.13**  Prove Proposition 8.19.

Let us now assume that $x$ is fixed. We investigate how to minimise $\text{AVaR}^\alpha(X_{(x,\mathbf{z})})$ by choosing $\mathbf{z}$. We assume that we invest $V_0$, which means that we can spend

$$c = V_0 - xS(0)$$

on put options. We assume that we do not take short positions in stock or puts, and that the total number of options does not exceed the number of shares of stock in our portfolio.

Under such assumptions, by (8.28), minimising $\text{AVaR}^\alpha(X_{(x,\mathbf{z})})$ is equivalent to the problem:

Find

$$\begin{aligned}
\min \ & \mathbf{z}^{\mathsf{T}}\mathbf{P}^\alpha, \\
\text{subject to:} \quad & \mathbf{z}^{\mathsf{T}}\mathbf{H}(0) = c, \\
& \mathbf{z}^{\mathsf{T}}\mathbf{1} \le x, \\
& z_0, \ldots, z_n \ge 0.
\end{aligned} \tag{8.29}$$

This is a linear programming problem, which can be solved numerically.

**Example 8.20**

Consider the Black–Scholes model with parameters $S(0) = 100$, $\mu = 10\%$, $\sigma = 0.2$ and $r = 3\%$. Assume that we spend $V_0 = 1000$, investing in stock and put options with strike prices $K_1 = 75$, $K_2 = 90$, $K_3 = 110$ and expiry $T = 1$. We shall solve the problem (8.29) for $\alpha = 0.05$, considering $c = 0, 10, 30, 50$ and $80$.

The choice of $x$ depends on $c$, since

$$xS(0) + c = V_0.$$

We compute the vectors $\mathbf{H}(0)$ and $\mathbf{P}^\alpha$ using (8.22) and (8.23), respectively,

$$\mathbf{H}(0) = \begin{bmatrix} 0.406 \\ 2.769 \\ 12.042 \end{bmatrix}, \qquad \mathbf{P}^\alpha = \begin{bmatrix} 0.140 \\ 0.819 \\ 1.724 \end{bmatrix}.$$

The solutions to the problem (8.29) are shown in the table:

| $c$ | $x$ | $z_1$ | $z_2$ | $z_3$ | $\text{AVaR}^\alpha$ |
|-----|-----|-------|-------|-------|------------------------|
| 0   | 10  | 0.00  | 0.00  | 0.00  | 302.24 |
| 10  | 9.9 | 7.37  | 2.53  | 0.00  | 242.61 |
| 30  | 9.7 | 0.00  | 9.36  | 0.34  | 146.23 |
| 50  | 9.5 | 0.00  | 6.95  | 2.55  | 120.68 |
| 80  | 9.2 | 0.00  | 3.32  | 5.88  | 82.35 |

From the table we can see that for larger $c$ we can afford to buy options with higher strike prices, which provide better protection, but are at the same time more expensive.

We finish the section by showing how to compute AVaR for investments in multiple assets. In such case a simple analytic formula for AVaR is not available and we make use of the Monte Carlo method discussed in (8.4).

**Example 8.21**
Consider the $n$-dimensional Black–Scholes market from Example 7.24. Using the same Monte Carlo simulation that was used to compute VaR in Example 7.24, we can compute the AVaR for the position using (8.4) and Corollary 8.6. We thus obtain $\text{AVaR}^\alpha(Y_N) = 61.75$ from the simulation.

---

**Exercise 8.14**   Recreate the numerical result from Example 8.21.

---

## 8.4 Coherence

In this section we provide an axiomatic description of a certain class of measures of risk. It will be apparent that this class contains AVaR, but not VaR.

By a risk measure we mean a number $\rho(X) \in \mathbb{R}$ that is assigned to a random variable $X$ to represent its risk. The following axioms are seen as natural requirements for a satisfactory risk measure.

**Definition 8.22**

A risk measure $\rho$ is **coherent** if it is:
  (i) monotone: $X \leq Y$ implies $\rho(X) \geq \rho(Y)$;
 (ii) cash-invariant: $\rho(X + m) = \rho(X) - m$;
(iii) positively homogeneous: for all $\lambda \geq 0, \rho(\lambda X) = \lambda \rho(X)$;
(iv) sub-additive: for any $X, Y$,

$$\rho(X + Y) \leq \rho(X) + \rho(Y).$$

Note that, by (ii), $\rho(X + \rho(X)) = 0$, so that $\rho(X)$ is the minimum amount of additional investment we need to add to $X$ to ensure that the final position eliminates risk, as measured by $\rho$. In other words,

$$\rho(X) = \inf\{m \in \mathbb{R} : \rho(X + m) \leq 0\}.$$

More generally, a position $X$ is said to be **acceptable** if $\rho(X) \leq 0$.

---

**Exercise 8.15** Show that if a risk measure $\rho$ satisfies (ii)–(iv) above, then it is monotone if and only if $X \geq 0$ implies $\rho(X) \leq 0$.

---

**Exercise 8.16** Show that any coherent risk measure $\rho$ is convex: for $\lambda \in [0, 1]$

$$\rho(\lambda X + (1 - \lambda)Y) \leq \lambda \rho(X) + (1 - \lambda)\rho(Y).$$

Show conversely that if a risk measure $\rho$ is convex and positively homogeneous, then it is coherent.

---

The following proposition describes a method of creating new coherent risk measures from an existing family of such measures, including convex combinations as a special case. We leave the simple proof as an exercise.

**Proposition 8.23**

*Given a family of coherent risk measures $\{\rho_\alpha : \alpha \in (0, 1)\}$ and a Borel probability measure $\mu$ on $(0, 1)$, then*

$$\rho_\mu(X) = \int_{(0,1)} \rho_\alpha(X) d\mu(\alpha)$$

*is a coherent risk measure.*

---

**Exercise 8.17**    Prove Proposition 8.23.

---

Motivated by the representation we found for AVaR$^\alpha$ we can immediately identify a large class of coherent risk measures by the following construction.

**Definition 8.24**

Suppose that $\mathcal{R}$ is a family of probability measures satisfying $\mathcal{R} \subset \{Q : Q \ll P\}$. We define a risk measure $\rho_{\mathcal{R}}$ by setting

$$\rho_{\mathcal{R}}(X) = \sup\{-\mathbb{E}_Q(X) : Q \in \mathcal{R}\}.$$

We show that $\rho_{\mathcal{R}}$ is indeed a coherent risk measure.

**Proposition 8.25**

*For any family $\mathcal{R}$ of probability measures absolutely continuous with respect to P,*

$$\rho_{\mathcal{R}}(X) = \sup\{-\mathbb{E}_Q(X) : Q \in \mathcal{R}\}$$

*defines a coherent risk measure.*

*Proof*   Given any probability measure $Q \ll P$, if $X \leq Y$ then $-\mathbb{E}_Q(X) \geq -\mathbb{E}_Q(Y)$, hence

$$\rho_{\mathcal{R}}(X) = \sup\{-\mathbb{E}_Q(X) : Q \in \mathcal{R}\} \geq \sup\{-\mathbb{E}_Q(Y) : Q \in \mathcal{R}\} = \rho_{\mathcal{R}}(Y).$$

If $m \in \mathbb{R}$, then since $\mathbb{E}_Q(X + m) = \mathbb{E}_Q(X) + m$

$$\begin{aligned}
\rho_{\mathcal{R}}(X + m) &= \sup\{-\mathbb{E}_Q(X + m) : Q \in \mathcal{R}\} \\
&= \sup\{-\mathbb{E}_Q(X) : Q \in \mathcal{R}\} - m \\
&= \rho_{\mathcal{R}}(X) - m.
\end{aligned}$$

We have $-\mathbb{E}_Q(\lambda X) = -\lambda \mathbb{E}_Q(X)$, so for $\lambda \geq 0$, taking the supremum over $Q$ in $\mathcal{R}$ gives $\rho_{\mathcal{R}}(\lambda X) = \lambda \rho_{\mathcal{R}}(X)$.

Finally, to prove sub-additivity, we use the fact that for two functions $f, g : U \to \mathbb{R}$, where $U$ is an arbitrary set,

$$\sup_{x \in U} \{f(x) + g(x)\} \leq \sup_{x \in U} f(x) + \sup_{x \in U} g(x). \tag{8.30}$$

Let us fix $X$ and $Y$. We apply (8.30) taking $U = \mathcal{R}$, $f(Q) = -\mathbb{E}_Q(X)$, and

$g(Q) = -\mathbb{E}_Q(Y)$. Thus

$$\begin{aligned}
\rho_{\mathcal{R}}(X + Y) &= \sup_{Q \in \mathcal{R}} \{-\mathbb{E}_Q(X + Y)\} \\
&= \sup_{Q \in \mathcal{R}} \{-\mathbb{E}_Q(X) - \mathbb{E}_Q(Y)\} \\
&\leq \sup_{Q \in \mathcal{R}} \{-\mathbb{E}_Q(X)\} + \sup_{Q \in \mathcal{R}} \{-\mathbb{E}_Q(Y)\} \qquad \text{(from 8.30)} \\
&= \rho_{\mathcal{R}}(X) + \rho_{\mathcal{R}}(Y),
\end{aligned}$$

as required. $\square$

AVaR was our first example of such a coherent risk measure: taking $\mathcal{R} = \mathcal{P}_\alpha = \left\{Q : Q \ll P, \frac{dQ}{dP} \leq \frac{1}{\alpha}\right\}$ gives AVaR$^\alpha$, as we saw in Theorem 8.10. We now consider some further examples.

**Example 8.26**
Take $\mathcal{R}_{\min} = \{P\}$, which gives $\rho_{\min} = -\mathbb{E}_P(X)$. This is a coherent risk measure by Proposition 8.25, but is not very useful. We see that if $\mathbb{E}_P(X) \geq 0$ then $\rho_{\min}(X)$ is negative, indicating that any random variable with positive expectation is acceptable.

**Example 8.27**
At the other extreme, we obtain a risk measure that is too stringent for practical use if we define

$$\rho_{\max}(X) = -\text{ess inf } X.$$

The right-hand side means that we can have $X(\omega) < -\text{ess inf } X$ only on a $P$-null set. The requirement $\rho_{\max}(X) \leq 0$ therefore means that this risk measure allows negative positions $X(\omega)$ only for a $P$-null set of $\omega$ in $\Omega$. Hence $\rho_{\max}(X) = \inf\{m \in \mathbb{R} : X + m \geq 0 \; P\text{-a.s.}\}$.

---

**Exercise 8.18** Show that $\rho_{\max}$ is coherent.

---

A potentially more useful risk measure is given by fixing $\alpha \in (0, 1)$ and taking $\mathcal{R}$ to include all conditional distributions $P(\cdot|A)$, as is done in the following definition.

**Definition 8.28**

Let

$$\mathcal{R}_\alpha = \left\{ Q_A | A \text{ is measurable, } P(A) > \alpha, \text{ and } Q_A(B) = P(B|A) = \frac{P(B \cap A)}{P(A)} \right\}.$$

We call

$$\mathrm{WCE}^\alpha(X) = \sup\{-\mathbb{E}_{Q_A}(X)|Q_A \in \mathcal{R}_\alpha\}$$

the **worst conditional expectation (WCE)** at level $\alpha$.

By its definition and Proposition 8.25, $\mathrm{WCE}^\alpha$ is a coherent risk measure.

---

**Exercise 8.19**  Consider the probability space $(\Omega, \mathcal{F}, P)$ and the random variables $X, Y$ defined in Example 8.13. Verify that $\mathrm{WCE}^\alpha(X) = \mathrm{WCE}^\alpha(Y) = 50$, and $\mathrm{AVaR}^\alpha(X) = \mathrm{AVaR}^\alpha(Y) = 60$, when $\alpha = 0.05$.

Verify that in this example, WCE is additive. Compare the risk measures VaR, TCE, WCE and AVaR for $X$.

---

We obtain the following inequalities from our definitions of risk measures explored so far (recall that $\mathrm{TCE}^\alpha$ and $\mathrm{WCE}^\alpha$ were defined in Definitions 8.12 and 8.28, respectively).

**Proposition 8.29**

*For any $X$ we have*

$$\mathrm{AVaR}^\alpha(X) \geq \mathrm{WCE}^\alpha(X) \geq \mathrm{TCE}^\alpha(X) \geq \mathrm{VaR}^\alpha(X).$$

*When $F_X$ is continuous at $\alpha$, the first three quantities coincide.*

*Proof*  Since

$$Q_A(B) = \frac{P(B \cap A)}{P(A)} = \frac{1}{P(A)} \int_B \mathbf{1}_A \, dP,$$

we see that

$$\frac{dQ_A}{dP} = \frac{\mathbf{1}_A}{P(A)}.$$

Taking any $A$ satisfying $P(A) > \alpha$, we see that $\frac{dQ_A}{dP} \leq \frac{1}{\alpha}$, so

$$Q_A \in \mathcal{P}_\alpha = \left\{ Q : Q \ll P, \frac{dQ}{dP} \leq \frac{1}{\alpha} \right\},$$

hence

$$\text{AVaR}^\alpha(X) = \sup_{Q \in \mathcal{P}_\alpha} \{-\mathbb{E}_Q(X)\} \geq \sup_{Q_A, P(A) > \alpha} \{-\mathbb{E}_{Q_A}(X)\} = \text{WCE}^\alpha(X).$$

This proves the first inequality.

For the second, let $\varepsilon > 0$ be given. Since $q^\alpha(X) = \inf\{x : F_X(x) > \alpha\}$ and $F_X$ is non-decreasing,

$$\alpha < P(X \leq q^\alpha(X) + \varepsilon),$$

so that $A_\varepsilon = \{X \leq q^\alpha(X) + \varepsilon\}$ has probability $P(A_\varepsilon) > \alpha$, which means that

$$\text{WCE}^\alpha(X) \geq -\mathbb{E}_{Q_{A_\varepsilon}}(X) = -\mathbb{E}(X | X \leq q^\alpha(X) + \varepsilon),$$

for all $\varepsilon > 0$. Letting $\varepsilon \downarrow 0$ we have $\text{WCE}^\alpha(X) \geq \text{TCE}^\alpha(X)$.

The final inequality follows by taking $B = \{X \leq -\text{VaR}^\alpha(X)\}$ and computing

$$
\begin{aligned}
\text{TCE}^\alpha(X) \; &= -\mathbb{E}(X | X \leq -\text{VaR}^\alpha(X)) && \text{(by 8.18)} \\
&= -\tfrac{1}{P(B)} \int_B X dP \\
&\geq -\tfrac{1}{P(B)} \int_B -\text{VaR}^\alpha(X) dP && \text{(on } B, \; X \leq -\text{VaR}^\alpha(X)) \\
&= \text{VaR}^\alpha(X). && \text{(since VaR}^\alpha(X) \text{ is a constant)}
\end{aligned}
$$

In (8.19) we have shown that when $F_X$ is continuous, $\text{AVaR}^\alpha(X) = \text{TCE}^\alpha(X)$, hence both equal $\text{WCE}^\alpha(X)$. □

One potential difficulty with AVaR is that it restricts attention to the $\alpha$-tail of the distribution function $F_X$ rather than taking the whole distribution of $X$ into account. Moreover, in taking averages it assigns the same weight to any $q^\beta(X)$ for $\beta < \alpha$. A natural route to more general risk measures is to assign different weights to different $\beta$.

**Definition 8.30**

Let $\varphi : (0, 1) \to \mathbb{R}$ be a non-negative, non-increasing function satisfying

$$\int_0^1 \varphi(x) dx = 1.$$

We define

$$\rho^\varphi(X) = -\int_0^1 q^\beta(X) \varphi(\beta) d\beta$$

as the **spectral risk measure** for $\varphi$.

**Example 8.31**

For $\alpha \in (0, 1)$ we recover AVaR$^\alpha(X)$ by choosing $\varphi(\beta) = \frac{1}{\alpha}\mathbf{1}_{[0,\alpha]}(\beta)$, since

$$-\int_0^1 q^\beta(X)\varphi(\beta)d\beta = -\frac{1}{\alpha}\int_0^\alpha q^\beta(X)d\beta = \text{AVaR}^\alpha(X).$$

The function $\varphi$ is also called a **risk-aversion function**, since it reflects the investor's attitude to risk by assigning weights (adding to 1) to the values in the distribution $F_X$. In the case of AVaR$^\alpha(X)$ these weights are simply uniformly distributed over the left $\alpha$-tail of $F_X$, and are zero elsewhere. The requirement that the weighting function $\varphi$ should be non-negative is obvious. That it is non-increasing suggests that a rational investor would be more concerned about worse outcomes in an assessment of risk. Thus a coherent risk measure should assign greater weight to worse potential outcomes.

**Theorem 8.32**

*A spectral risk measure $\rho^\varphi$ is coherent.*

*Proof* We recast $\rho^\varphi$ in the form $\rho_\mu$ as defined in Proposition 8.23, which will prove coherence. For this, we consider the family $\{\rho_\alpha; \alpha \in (0, 1)\}$ of coherent risk measures with $\rho_\alpha = \text{AVaR}^\alpha$ and construct an appropriate probability measure $\mu$ on $(0, 1)$.

First, given a function $\varphi$ as in Definition 8.30, define a set function $\nu$ on intervals in $(0, 1)$ by letting, for $0 < x < 1$,

$$\nu((x, 1)) = \varphi(x). \tag{8.31}$$

and, for $0 < a < b < 1$, setting $\nu((a, b]) = \varphi(a) - \varphi(b)$. This defines $\nu$ as an additive set function on intervals $(a, b] \subset (0, 1)$, which extends to a unique measure $\nu$ on all Borel sets $A$ in $(0, 1)$. Now set

$$\mu(A) = \int_A x d\nu(x).$$

For pairs $(x, y)$, read the inequalities $0 < y < x < 1$ from left to right and right to left respectively, to obtain

$$\mathbf{1}_{(0,x)}(y) = \mathbf{1}_{(y,1)}(x). \tag{8.32}$$

Hence, using Fubini's theorem, we obtain

$$\mu((0,1)) = \int_{(0,1)} x\, d\nu(x)$$

$$= \int_{(0,1)} \left( \int_{(0,1)} \mathbf{1}_{(0,x)}(y)\, dy \right) d\nu(x)$$

$$= \int_{(0,1)} \left( \int_{(0,1)} \mathbf{1}_{(0,x)}(y)\, d\nu(x) \right) dy \qquad \text{(Fubini's theorem)}$$

$$= \int_{(0,1)} \left( \int_{(0,1)} \mathbf{1}_{(y,1)}(x)\, d\nu(x) \right) dy \qquad \text{(by (8.32))}$$

$$= \int_{(0,1)} \left( \int_{(y,1)} d\nu(x) \right) dy$$

$$= \int_{(0,1)} \varphi(y)\, dy \qquad \text{(by (8.31))}$$

$$= 1. \qquad \text{(by Definition 8.30)}$$

Hence $\mu$ is a probability measure on $(0,1)$, so that $\rho_\mu$ is coherent by Proposition 8.23.

We have $d\mu(\alpha) = \alpha\, d\nu(\alpha)$, and

$$\rho_\mu(X) = \int_{(0,1)} \text{AVaR}^\alpha(X)\, d\mu(\alpha)$$

$$= \int_{(0,1)} \text{AVaR}^\alpha(X)\alpha\, d\nu(\alpha)$$

$$= \int_{(0,1)} \left( -\int_{(0,\alpha)} q^\beta(X)\, d\beta \right) d\nu(\alpha)$$

$$= -\int_{(0,1)} \left( \int_{(0,1)} \mathbf{1}_{(0,\alpha)}(\beta)q^\beta(X)\, d\beta \right) d\nu(\alpha)$$

$$= -\int_{(0,1)} \left( \int_{(0,1)} \mathbf{1}_{(0,\alpha)}(\beta)q^\beta(X)\, d\nu(\alpha) \right) d\beta \qquad \text{(Fubini's theorem)}$$

$$= -\int_{(0,1)} q^\beta(X) \left( \int_{(0,1)} \mathbf{1}_{(\beta,1)}(\alpha)\, d\nu(\alpha) \right) d\beta \qquad \text{(by (8.32))}$$

$$= -\int_{(0,1)} q^\beta(X) \left( \int_{(\beta,1)} d\nu(\alpha) \right) d\beta$$

$$= -\int_{(0,1)} q^\beta(X)\varphi(\beta)\, d\beta \qquad \text{(by (8.31))}$$

$$= \rho^\varphi(X),$$

hence the theorem is proved. $\qquad\qquad\qquad\qquad\qquad\qquad\qquad\qquad\qquad$ □

The flexibility inherent in the choice of $\varphi$ means that individual's subjective risk profiles can be mapped onto spectral risk measures to obtain different assessments of risk. We content ourselves with just one example.

**Example 8.33**

Recall the exponential utility function $u(x) = -e^{-ax}$ introduced in Chapter 6, where $a$ is the investor's absolute risk aversion coefficient. We obtain the corresponding weighting function in the form $\varphi(x) = ke^{-ax}$, since with $k > 0$ we have $\varphi \geq 0$ and $\varphi$ is (strictly) decreasing on $[0, 1]$. To ensure that it is an admissible risk spectrum, we simply need to choose $k$ such that $\int_0^1 \varphi(t)dt = 1$, which forces $k = \frac{a}{1-e^{-a}}$. The spectral risk measure

$$\rho^\varphi(X) = \frac{a}{1 - e^{-a}} \int_{(0,1)} (-q^\beta(X))e^{-a\beta}d\beta$$

thus takes account of the investor's risk aversion by giving most weight to the worst outcomes.

## 8.5  Proofs

**Lemma 8.4**

*Let $X : \Omega \to \mathbb{R}$ be a random variable. Assume that $U$ is a uniformly distributed random variable on $(0, 1)$. Then the random variable $Y$, defined by $Y(x) = q^{U(x)}(X)$, has the same distribution as $X$.*

*Proof*   Let us use a notation $g : (0, 1) \to \mathbb{R}$ for

$$g(\alpha) = q^\alpha(X).$$

Then $Y = g(U)$.

Since $U$ is a uniformly distributed random variable on $(0, 1)$, for any Borel set $A \subset (0, 1)$ the probability that $U$ is in $A$ is

$$\text{Prob}(U \in A) = m(A),$$

where $m$ stands for the Lebesgue measure.

Let $y \in \mathbb{R}$ be fixed. There can exist at most one $\alpha$ such that

$$g(\alpha) = q^\alpha(X) = y.$$

(There is a possibility that such $\alpha$ does not exist. This is when $y$ lies below the flat part of the distribution function $F_X(y)$; see Figure 7.1 on page 100.) This means that the pre-image $g^{-1}(y)$ consists of at most a single point,

hence

$$\text{Prob}(g(U) = y) = \text{Prob}(U \in g^{-1}(y)) = m(g^{-1}(y)) = 0. \tag{8.33}$$

By the definition of the upper quantile, i.e.

$$q^{\alpha}(X) = \inf\{x : \alpha < F_X(x)\}, \tag{8.34}$$

we see that if $\alpha < F_X(x)$ then $q^{\alpha}(X) \leq x$. This means that

$$\{\alpha : \alpha < F_X(y)\} \subset \{\alpha : q^{\alpha}(X) \leq y\} = \{\alpha : g(\alpha) \leq y\}, \tag{8.35}$$

hence

$$\begin{aligned}
F_Y(y) &= \text{Prob}\,(Y \leq y) \\
&= \text{Prob}(g(U) \leq y) \\
&\geq \text{Prob}(U < F_X(y)) \quad \text{(by (8.35))} \\
&= F_X(y).
\end{aligned}$$

Again, by the definition of $q^{\alpha}(X)$ (see (8.34)), we see that if $q^{\alpha}(X) < x$ then $\alpha < F_X(x)$, hence

$$\{\alpha : g(\alpha) < y\} = \{\alpha : q^{\alpha}(X) < y\} \subset \{\alpha : \alpha < F_X(y)\}. \tag{8.36}$$

This gives

$$\begin{aligned}
F_Y(y) &= \text{Prob}\,(Y \leq y) \\
&= \text{Prob}(g(U) \leq y) \\
&= \text{Prob}(g(U) < y) + \text{Prob}(g(U) = y) \\
&= \text{Prob}(g(U) < y) \quad \text{(by (8.33))} \\
&\leq \text{Prob}(U < F_X(y)) \quad \text{(by (8.36))} \\
&= F_X(y).
\end{aligned}$$

We have shown that $F_Y(y) = F_X(y)$, which concludes our proof. $\qquad\square$

**Corollary 8.7**
*If $X$ is a random variable whose distribution function $F_X$ is strictly increasing and continuous, then*

$$\text{AVaR}^{\alpha}(X) = -\mathbb{E}(X | X \leq q^{\alpha}(X)).$$

*Proof* Since $F_X$ is continuous, for any $q \in \mathbb{R}$,

$$P(X = q) = 0. \tag{8.37}$$

By Lemma 7.5

$$q^{\alpha}(X) = F_X^{-1}(\alpha), \tag{8.38}$$

hence

$$P(X < q^\alpha(X)) = P(X \le q^\alpha(X)) - P(X = q^\alpha(X))$$
$$= P(X \le q^\alpha(X)) \quad \text{(using (8.37))} \quad (8.39)$$
$$= F_X(q_\alpha(X))$$
$$= \alpha. \quad \text{(using (8.38))}$$

Substituting into (8.2) gives

$$\text{AVaR}^\alpha(X) = -\frac{1}{\alpha} \left[ \mathbb{E}(X\mathbf{1}_{\{X<q^\alpha(X)\}}) + q^\alpha(X)(\alpha - P(X < q^\alpha(X))) \right]$$
$$= -\frac{1}{\alpha} \mathbb{E}(X\mathbf{1}_{\{X<q^\alpha(X)\}})$$
$$= -\frac{1}{\alpha} \mathbb{E}(X\mathbf{1}_{\{X\le q^\alpha(X)\}}) \quad \text{(since by (8.37), } P(X = q^\alpha(X)) = 0)$$
$$= -\frac{1}{P(X \le q^\alpha(X))} \mathbb{E}(X\mathbf{1}_{\{X\le q^\alpha(X)\}}) \quad \text{(from (8.38))}$$
$$= -\mathbb{E}(X|X \le q^\alpha(X)),$$

as required.                                                                                                    □

## Lemma 8.8

*For $\alpha \in (0, 1)$, let $q^\alpha = q^\alpha(X)$ and set*

$$\mathbf{1}_X^\alpha = \begin{cases} \mathbf{1}_{\{X<q^\alpha\}} & \text{if } P(X = q^\alpha) = 0, \\ \mathbf{1}_{\{X<q^\alpha\}} + \kappa\mathbf{1}_{\{X=q^\alpha\}} & \text{if } P(X = q^\alpha) > 0, \end{cases}$$

*where $\kappa = \frac{\alpha - P(X<q^\alpha)}{P(X=q^\alpha)}$. Then*

$$\mathbb{E}(\mathbf{1}_X^\alpha) = \alpha, \quad (8.40)$$

*and for all $\omega \in \Omega$,*

$$\mathbf{1}_X^\alpha(\omega) \in [0, 1].$$

*Proof*  For (8.40) observe that if $P(X = q^\alpha) = 0$ then

$$\mathbb{E}(\mathbf{1}_X^\alpha) = P(X < q^\alpha) = P(X \le q^\alpha) = \alpha,$$

while if $P(X > q^\alpha) > 0$ we have

$$\mathbb{E}(\mathbf{1}_X^\alpha) = P(X < q^\alpha) + \alpha - P(X < q^\alpha) = \alpha.$$

To prove the second claim we start by observing that when $P(X = q^\alpha) = 0$, then $\mathbf{1}_X^\alpha = \mathbf{1}_{\{X<q^\alpha\}} \in \{0, 1\}$. If $P(X = q^\alpha) > 0$ and $\omega \notin \{X = q^\alpha\}$ then

$$\mathbf{1}_X^\alpha(\omega) = \mathbf{1}_{\{X<q^\alpha\}}(\omega) \in \{0, 1\}.$$

The only non-trivial case is when $P(X = q^\alpha) > 0$ and $\omega \in \{X = q^\alpha\}$.

In such a case (using the standard notation $F_X(x_-) = \lim_{y \nearrow x} F_X(y)$),

$$P(X = q^\alpha) = F_X(q^\alpha) - F_X(q^\alpha_-),$$

so that for $\omega \in \{X = q^\alpha\}$,

$$\mathbf{1}^\alpha_X(\omega) = \kappa = \frac{\alpha - F_X(q^\alpha_-)}{F_X(q^\alpha) - F_X(q^\alpha_-)}. \tag{8.41}$$

By definition

$$q^\alpha = \inf\{x : \alpha < F_X(x)\},$$

and we see that for any $q < q^\alpha$ we have $\alpha \geq F_X(q)$, hence

$$\alpha \geq F_X(q^\alpha_-).$$

For any $q > q^\alpha$, $\alpha < F_X(q)$, and by right continuity of $F_X$ we have

$$\alpha \leq F_X(q^\alpha).$$

We have shown that $\alpha \in [F_X(q^\alpha_-), F_X(q^\alpha)]$, hence the quotient from (8.41) lies in $[0, 1]$. $\qquad\square$

# Index

Printed in the United States
by Baker & Taylor Publisher Services